JOYCE'S INVESTMENTS

A STORY FOR GIRLS

FANNIE E. NEWBERRY

1st WORLD
LIBRARY
Literary Society

Joyce's Investments

Fannie E. Newberry

© 1st World Library, 2007
PO Box 2211
Fairfield, IA 52556
www.1stworldlibrary.com
First Edition

LCCN: 2007934128

Softcover ISBN: 978-1-4218-9640-3
Hardcover ISBN: 978-1-4218-9740-0
eBook ISBN: 978-1-4218-9540-6

Purchase *"Joyce's Investments"*
as a traditional bound book at:
www.1stWorldLibrary.com/purchase.asp?ISBN=978-1-4218-9640-3

1st World Library is a literary, educational organization
dedicated to:

- Creating a free internet library of downloadable ebooks

- Hosting writing competitions and offering book publishing
  scholarships.

1st World Library Literary Society

Giving Back to the World

"If you want to work on the core problem, it's early school literacy."

- James Barksdale, former CEO of Netscape

"No skill is more crucial to the future of a child, or to a democratic and prosperous society, than literacy."

- Los Angeles Times

"Literacy... means far more than learning how to read and write... The aim is to transmit... knowledge and promote social participation."

- UNESCO

"Literacy is not a luxury, it is a right and a responsibility. If our world is to meet the challenges of the twenty-first century we must harness the energy and creativity of all our citizens."

- President Bill Clinton

"Parents should be encouraged to read to their children, and teachers should be equipped with all available techniques for teaching literacy, so the varying needs and capacities of individual kids can be taken into account."

- Hugh Mackay

"Women have the genius of charity,
A man gives but his gold;
Woman adds to it her sympathy."

CONTENTS

CHAPTER I

LEGAL ADVICE

The old lawyer caressed his smoothly shaven chin and gazed out at Joyce Lavillotte from under his shaggy eyebrows, as from the port-holes of a castle, impressing her as being quite as inscrutable of aspect and almost as belligerent. She, flushed and bright-eyed, leaned forward with an appealing air, opposing the resistless vigor of youth to the impassiveness of age.

"It is not the crazy scheme you think it, Mr. Barrington," she said in that liquid voice which was an inheritance from her creole ancestry, "and I do not mean to risk my last dollar. You know I have means that cannot be touched. Why should you be so sure I cannot manage the Works—especially when Mr. Dalton is so capable and—"

The lawyer uttered something between a grunt and a laugh.

"It's Mr. Dalton who will manage it all. What do you know of the Works?"

"No, he will not, Mr. Barrington. The factory, of course, is his province, but the village shall be mine. You think, because I am not yet twenty-two, that I do not know my own mind, but you forget how long I have been motherless; and a girl has to think for herself when her mother goes."

"But your father?"

"You knew my father." The tremble in the young voice hardened into a haughty note, and she drew back coldly.

Mr. Barrington heaved a perplexed sigh.

"I know I ought to oppose you to the death, even! You'll never have such another chance to sell out, and the sum safely invested in bonds and mortgages, would keep you like a princess."

"I don't want to be kept like a princess. I don't choose to make use of that money for myself, Mr. Barrington—I can't. There is enough of my mother's for my few needs. I was brought up simply, and I am glad! If I sell the works, as you desire, I shall still give the proceeds away. Had you rather I built a hospital, or founded a girl's college, or set up a mission to the South Pole? I'd rather build a town on rational principles."

The haughtiness had melted now, and the smile with which she ended was hard to resist. A younger man would have yielded sooner, but Mr. Barrington was a sharp, practical financier, and furthermore, he had what he believed to be the best good of his client at heart. She was of age and, under the conditions of her late father's will, absolute mistress of a great fortune. It was aggravating to find she had no intention of sitting down to enjoy this in a comfortable, lady-like manner, but must at once begin to develope schemes and plans which seemed half insane to him. Why should this new generation of women be so streaked with quirks and oddities, so knobby with ideas, when they might be just as helpless

Fannie E. Newberry

and charming as those of his own day, and give themselves blindly to the guidance of astute men like himself? It was maddening to contemplate. Here was one who could be clothed in purple and fine linen and fare sumptuously every day, without so much as lifting her little white finger, and she was planning an infinity of care and worriment, possibly the loss of everything, rather than a calm acceptance of her rosy fortune. It fairly disgusted him!

His vis-a-vis, watching him with her keen dark eyes, read these thoughts as if his brain had been a printed page before her, and in spite of herself laughed outright; in his very teeth—a merry little peal as spontaneous as a sunburst.

"Pardon me!" she begged, trying vainly to control herself, "but you did look so hopeless, Mr. Harrington. I know I'm a nuisance to you, and I appreciate that this solicitude for my interests is more than I've any right to expect when I disappoint you so. If you were not so old a friend I wouldn't feel so guilty. Yet in spite of all—I am resolved."

She said the last three words quite gently, with a level gaze that met his own frowning one and held it. She did not nod nor bridle, and her air was almost deprecating in its modesty, but he felt the battle was over and she was the victor. She would be her own mistress, girl that she was, and he could not turn her. He leaned back in a relaxed attitude and asked in a changed voice, "Will you then care to retain the services of Barrington and Woodstock?"

There was not a hint of triumph in tone or manner as she answered quickly,

"Most certainly, if I may. There will be a constant need of your advice, I know. And now, Mr. Barrington, shall we settle the matter of salary, or do you prefer to make a separate charge for each occasion?"

His smile was rather grim as he arose and took down a bundle of papers and documents, slipped them rapidly from hand to hand, then laid them in order before him.

"I think the salary might be best for you," he answered.

"So do I," blithely, "for I shall probably bore you to death!"

This matter having been satisfactorily adjusted, the lawyer, with a rather ironical air, observed,

"If I am not trenching upon forbidden ground, might I ask a few more questions concerning this scheme of yours?"

"As many as you like, sir."

"Thank you. I take it for granted you will retain Mr. Dalton as manager?"

"Yes."

"And most of the employees as at present?"

"All, for aught I know."

"And you speak of building up a town—just what does that mean to your own mind?"

"I'll try to tell you. You know at present there are only the buildings for the Works, the branch track and engine sheds, and the few rows of uncomfortable cottages for the families of the men. There is no school, no church, no library, no meeting-place of any kind, except the grocery store and saloon; and those bare, staring rows of mean houses, just

Fannie E. Newberry

alike, are not homes in any sense of the word. I want to add all such comforts—no, I call them necessities—and more."

"More? As what, for instance?"

"Well,"—she drew a long breath and settled back in her chair with a nestling movement that made the hard man of business feel a certain fatherly yearning towards her, and at last said slowly, "I can't quite explain to you how I have been led to it, but this thought has become very plain to me—that every real need of humanity must (if this world be the work of a perfect Being) have its certain fulfilment. Most people think the fulfilment should only be looked for in another and better world. I think it might, and ought, to come often in this, and that we alone are to blame that it does not."

"Wait! Let me more fully understand. You think every need—what kind of needs?"

"All kinds. Needs of body, mind, and soul."

"You think they can be fully gratified here?"

"I think they might be. I believe there is no reason, except our own ignorance, stupidity, prejudice, and greed, that keeps them from being gratified here and now."

"But child—that would be Heaven!"

"Very like it—yes. And why shouldn't we have Heaven here, sir? God made this world and pronounced it good. Would the Perfect One make a broken circle, a chain with missing links, a desire without its gratification? That would be incomplete workmanship. When either my body or my soul calls out for anything whatsoever, somewhere there is that thing awaiting the desire. Why relegate it to another world? There must be complete circles here, or this world is not good."

"But, my dear girl, these are rather abstruse questions for your little head."

"I did not think them out, Mr. Barrington. They grew out of—circumstances—and some one a good deal wiser than I made me understand them. But they grew to stay, and I can't get rid of them. That is one of the thoughts, ideas—what you will, and this is the other. A man can do little alone, but men can do anything working together in perfect sympathy."

"Oh, co-operation—yes!"

"Co-operation, as you say. With perfect co-operation and a perfect communication, so that each need may be answered readily—these are the ideas I wish to work out."

"Work out—how?"

"In my village."

He frowned at her in puzzled petulance.

"I don't understand a word."

"And it's almost impossible to make one understand, sir. Just wait and watch the working of my plan. Mr. Barrington, have you ever had a surplus of anything that you would gladly share with another, if you knew exactly where it was most needed?"

"Yes," smiling suddenly, and glancing into a corner where was a heaped-up, disorderly looking set of shelves from which the books had overflowed upon the floor. "I was thinking, the other day, that if I knew just the right young

Fannie E. Newberry

lawyer I would be glad to give him some of those Reports."

"That's it! That's what I mean. Somewhere, some struggling lawyer is longing for books and cannot get them; you have too many and are longing to be rid of them. There are the two halves of a complete whole; don't you see?"

"Certainly—if they could be brought together."

"Well, I want to try and bring them together."

"In your village? But how? Do you imagine you can play Providence to a whole settlement, and complete all its half circles?"

"No, sir, I've no thought of that. I simply want to make it possible for them to play Providence to each other. But it would take all day to tell you just how. You have a clue now, and suppose you watch me work it out. I shall probably come to you often for advice, and I must not take up more of your time to-day."

She arose, with a brisk movement, and began fastening her fur collar, in spite of his detaining gesture.

"No, no," she laughed, "don't tempt me! When I mount my hobby it carries me fast and far. Save yourself from its heels. But I will come again."

He laughed with a hearty note.

"You know when to dismount, evidently, and just in time to whet one's curiosity, too. I may be asking to ride it myself, next. Well, do come again—but wait! What's the name of your new town?"

"I've been puzzling over that, Mr. Barrington. I wanted in some way to have my family name connected with it, and yet not so distinctly as to be suggestive, either. There is the English of it—of course it's a free translation—that might do. I don't care to hint at my ideas in the name, so perhaps—"

"Lavillotte?" he questioned. "What is the English of it."

"'The little town,' but Littletown—"

"Why not drop the w?"

"And make it Littleton? Well, why not? I rather like that! It seems impersonal; it explains nothing."

"Except its smallness," laughed the lawyer, "and that would be apparent anyhow, I suppose."

She laughed with him.

"I'm afraid so. Yes, I believe it will do. Littleton! It really suits me."

"There! Didn't I tell you? I've named your model town already; I shall be galloping side by side with you before you know it. Off with you now, hobby and all!"

But she passed out smiling and satisfied. When Mr. Barrington took that tone she knew he was the old friend again, and not the legal adviser; and much as she respected the lawyer, she far preferred the friend, to-day.

Fannie E. Newberry

CHAPTER II

OLD FRIENDS

Miss Lavillotte descended in the elevator and hurried out to her waiting brougham, and stopped an instant with her foot on the step, to turn a kindly, inquiring gaze upon the elderly coachman, who held the door open before her. An amused twinkle grew in his honest eyes as he gravely responded to the glance with the words, "No, Miss Joyce, I'm not tired nor cold—where next?"

"If you are certain, Gilbert; but it was a good while, and"— "It's mild and pleasant to-day, Miss Joyce."

"Well, it's good of you to think so. Then drive to the Bonnivels, and I won't be so long this time."

"Take all the time you want, Miss Joyce."

He gently shut the door upon her and, mounting to the box, drove carefully away through the thronged streets, turning westward and leaving the neighborhood of legal offices to plunge into the somewhat unsavory precincts given over to markets and fruit venders, passing which, he gradually emerged into the less frequented lengths of avenue leading far out into the suburbs. It was a long and not too pleasant drive, but Joyce Lavillotte was too busy with her thoughts to mind, and Gilbert Judson too intent upon the safe guidance of her spirited team to care. The dreamer inside was indeed surprised when he stopped and, glancing out, she saw they had reached their destination.

It was a corner house, frame-built, and of a comfortable, unfashionable aspect, set down in a square which showed its well-kept green even in winter. The lace-hung windows were broad, sunny and many paned, and a gilded cage flashed back the light in one of them. Joyce flung it an eager glance of expectancy and ran lightly up the steps of the square porch, as if overjoyed to be there. Before she could ring, the door was flung open with the outburst,

"I knowed it was you! I saw you froo de window." She caught up the laughing child with a loving word. "Of course you knew me, sweetheart! Where's mama, and Auntie, and 'Wobin', and all?"

The brown curls bobbed against her shoulder and the red lips met her own in frank affection.

"Dey's heah, but Wobin's wunned away."

"Wunned away? The naughty dog! Ah, Dorette, there you are! How's the blessed mother?"

"Better, Joyce; no pain in several days. Come in, dear—she'll be so glad! Oh, Joyce I did think when all restrictions were removed—"

"Ah! no, dear. You knew I would observe every form of respect. I have been nowhere yet."

She glanced down meaningly at her black gown, and

Fannie E. Newberry

Dorette's olive skin flushed in a delicate fashion.

"I beg your pardon. You are right, as usual. Come in to ma mere."

Joyce followed the sweet-faced young woman, still carrying the little child who was so like her, and thus entered the large and pleasant living-room of the old house. In the embrasure of one broad window, seeming to focus all the light which streamed in freely through the thin, parted curtains, sat a woman in a gown of soft white wool, made with artistic simplicity. Her face had the same soft cream tint as her gown, and the hair, turned back in loose waves from her broad forehead, was of a purplish black, occasionally streaked with gray. All the features were clean-cut and delicate, but the expression in the large black eyes was that vague, appealing one which too surely indicates the utter loss of sight.

Evidently the woman, still exceptionally beautiful in her maturity, was hopelessly blind.

Joyce quickly set down the little one, and advanced on winged feet.

"Ma mere," she said in a voice almost of adoration, as she dropped to her knees beside the woman's chair, "Ma mere, I have come back."

"Dear one! Ma petite!" exclaimed the other in liquid southern accents, reaching out a delicate, trembling hand, which the girl caught and kissed devotedly. "We have longed for you. But we knew you would come! Let me see your face, child."

Joyce turned it upward and remained very still while the

other lightly touched brow, eyes, lips, and chin, in a swift, assured fashion.

"Ah, you are truly the same little Joyce. There is the breadth between the eyes like an innocent child's, the straight, firm little nose like a Greek outline, the full curved lips—do you still pout when angry, cherie?—and that square, decided turn to the chin, more apparent than ever. You have grown, Joyce; you are a woman now."

"Yes, mother, but still a baby to you, and I want always to keep the old name for you, no matter how I grow. Ma mere, you have grown younger, and are more beautiful than ever."

"No flattery, mignonne! It is not good for me. Sit down here and tell us all there is to tell. You are very lonely, now?"

"I am alone—yes."

Joyce drew a chair close beside the other and sat down, while the older women smiled slightly.

"Yes, there is a difference. They tell me you are very rich."

"Too rich, dear mother; it frightens me!"

"Money is a great power, my child."

"And a terrible responsibility, as you have always taught me, ma mere."

"True. We have both known happy days without it. Still—"
"If it had only come in the right way, Mother Bonnivel!" cried the girl in an irrepressible outburst, "But oh! there's a stain on every dollar. I must spend my whole life trying to remove the stain, trying to make it honest money. Do you

remember our little French fable? How the cursed coin of the oppressor left its mark in boils and burns, until it had been sanctified by relieving the starving child? I must sanctify what my father—snatched—ma mere."

"And you will, Joyce—I know that."

"Yes, I mean to, God helping me. I have just come from a stormy interview with dear old Mr. Barrington, but I have won him over at last. Yet, it is you, mother, who will do it all, for I shall simply carry out your plans and—"

"My plans? what, Joyce! I have never—"

"Oh no, because you had not the means, so what was the use? But all the same it is you. Didn't you supply all the ideas, all the longings and the foresight? Every bit of it is what you have instilled into me from babyhood."

"They are your own dreams—yours and Leon's. Now let us make them reality. But where did Dorette go, and where is Camille? I want you all to hear—and good Larry, too."

"Then stay the day with us, dear. Larrimer will not be home till evening, and there is so much to talk about."

"Shall I? Oh, how blissful to think I can! I will go out and send Gilbert home, then. He has waited for me so patiently all the morning. Dear Mother Bonnivel, is it wicked that I can't be sad and regretful, but that the freedom is so sweet—*so sweet*?"

"It is natural at least, my love. Go and dismiss Gilbert until to-morrow morning. It will be too late for your long ride home after our seven o'clock dinner. Then hurry back. I begrudge every minute you are gone."

Joyce sped gaily away, and returned minus her hat and furs.

"I left them in the hall," she explained, as Dorette looked up questioningly, having just re-entered. "Are you glad I'm to stay, Dodo? Do give me some sewing now, Dorey, just in the old way. Is there nothing to do for baby?"

"Nothing! Indeed you'd think there was something, to see the way she goes through her clothing. She's a perfect terror, Joyce! Well, take this bit of a yoke—can you hemstitch as neatly as ever?"

"Try me; I don't know. Ellen does everything now."

"You have a maid?"

"Oh yes, I could not live alone. But Ellen is scarcely that. She is too staid, too old and respectable. She is my companion, rather."

"And you are still in that great hotel?"

"Yes, our rooms were taken for a year, and the time is not up for some months yet, so it seemed best. And we are quite independent there. We live as quietly in our suite of rooms as if we were in a separate flat. And our places at table are reserved in a far corner of the great salon, so that by timing ourselves we avoid the crowd, and we do not become conspicuous."

"Yes, I understand. One can live much as one elects to anywhere," said Madame Bonnivel, caressing little Dodo as the child leaned against her.

"I don't know," laughed Joyce. "There have been times when we didn't think so—did we, Dorette? Oh, it is so good—so

Fannie E. Newberry

good to be here!"

Over their needle-work the talk ran on, largely reminiscent in character, and mostly in a joyous strain. The young matron, Mrs. Larrimer Driscoll, was evidently no ready talker, but her interest was so vivid that she was a constant incitement to Joyce, who seemed to have broken bounds, and was by turns grave and gay, imperious and pleading in a succession of moods as natural as a child's and almost as little controlled. Presently she who has been referred to as Dodo's auntie, Miss Camille Bonnivel, entered and, after one swift look at the guest, who stood smilingly awaiting the outbreak of her astonishment, threw up both hands and flew across the room.

"Joyce!" she cried, "Joyce Lavillotte! So the proud heiress of a hundred acres—mostly marsh-land, but no matter!—has condescended to our low estate. Shall I go down on one knee, or two?"

"On four, if you have them, you gypsy! Come, kiss me and stop this nonsense. Dear! How you have grown, you tiny thing. You must be nearly to my elbows by this."

"Elbows! I'm well on towards five feet, I'll let you know. But you are superb, Joyce—'divinely tall and most divinely fair'; isn't that it? Come, stoop to me."

They kissed heartily, the dark little creature standing on tiptoe, while Joyce bent her head low, then Dodo claimed attention from "Cammy," and amid bursts of laughter and sometimes a rush of sudden tears, the talk flowed on, as it can only flow when dearest friends meet after long separation, with no estrangement and no doubts to dim the charms of renewed intercourse.

CHAPTER III

JOYCE'S INTERESTS

Joyce had not exaggerated when she spoke of the settlement about the Works as a desolate, unpicturesque, uninviting spot, and Camille had skirted the truth, at least, when she referred to the inherited acres as "marsh lands." Had she named them a desert instead, though, she would have been nearer correct, for is not a desert a "great sandy plain?" So was the site of the great factories known as the Early Glass Works. They seemed to have been set down with no thought but to construct—a shelter for costly machinery; as to those who worked it, let them manage anyhow. The buildings were massive and expensive where used to protect senseless iron and steel; low, squalid, and flung together in the cheapest way where used to house sentient human beings.

In a certain spasm of reformation they had been purchased by James J. Early after a venture in his gambling schemes so surpassingly "lucky"—to quote himself—that he was almost shamed into decency by its magnitude. He even felt a thrill of compunction—a very brief thrill—for the manner in which two-score people, who had trusted him, were left in the trough of ruin while he rode high on the wave of success. Almost trembling between triumph and contrition, he had been seized with the virtuous resolve to quit speculation for

Fannie E. Newberry

honest industry, and his investment in these glass-works was the result. Through his wildest plunging he had been shrewd enough never to risk his all in one venture—in fact, he never took any great risks for himself, except so far as his immortal soul was concerned—consequently when death overtook him and he, perforce, laid down the only thing he valued, his fortune, it had reached proportions of which figures could give but little idea. His daughter Joyce, sole heir-at-law, was almost overwhelmed by the burden of these millions, especially as she realized how dishonestly they had been acquired. She thoroughly appreciated the methods taken to possess them (one cannot say earn in this connection) and her sensitive soul shrank in terror from benefiting only through others' misfortunes. If she could not gather up and restore, she might at least bestow wherever help seemed most needed, thus perhaps in time lifting the curse she felt must rest on these ill-gotten gains. With James Early's usual policy he had spent money at the Works only where it would increase the value of the plant, and the working power of the machinery. The idea of wasting a dollar in making the homes of his employees more attractive, or in putting within their reach mental and moral helps, had never even occurred to him. Treeless, arid, and flat, the country stretched away on every side, only broken by one or two slight knolls separating the Works from a small river that intersected the land at some distance. In the midst of this plain stood the great buildings, belching forth smoke from their tall chimneys, while, radiating from this busy nucleus, were several rows of mere barracks, known as the cottages of the workmen.

It should be the daughter's policy to make this district blossom as the rose, and to make its people happy and contented.

You have doubtless noticed the seeming discrepancy between the names borne by Joyce and her father, and this is its explanation. The marriage of the scheming Yankee, James Early, into the then wealthy and powerful family of Lavillotte, old-timers of Louisiana soil, was considered the opposite of an honor by them, with the exception of the young girl, educated in the north, who had been fascinated by his fine looks and glib tongue. Therefore, when Joyce was born, an edict was issued by its leading members—two patriarchal uncles who held control of the property—that she should be cut off from her maternal rights in the family estate unless allowed to take the family name. Now, the loss of money was to J. J. Early the only loss worth mentioning, so he reluctantly consented, with but one stipulation—that she should bear his middle name, which was Joyce. Having assured themselves that Joyce was a proper Christian cognomen, suitable to a woman, they yielded the point, and Joyce Early was made Joyce Lavillotte by due process of law before old enough to know, much less to speak, her name. That this property was largely lost during the civil war, leaving the Earlys almost destitute at the time that broken-spirited lady died, had never altered this fact; nor was it changed when, later, after the death of both uncles, the property in partially restored shape came to the girl, so bound beneath legal restrictions, that she could never have the management of anything but the income. In fact, so engrossed had Early become in his own money-making, by this, that he had little thought to bestow upon a daughter who could never sympathize in what made life's interest for him. He had controlled her existence to his own purposes, knowing that an acknowledged home and daughter somehow give a man caste in the community, but outside of certain restrictions, and very galling ones, he had let her severely alone. Now that liberty and great means had fallen to her, what use should she make of them?

She stood a moment looking around her, after she had alighted from the train at the little brown one-room

Fannie E. Newberry

station-house, trying to take it all in at one glance of her brilliant eyes. She had never been here before, but she had had countless photographs made, and supposed herself thoroughly acquainted with the spot. But, to some minds, photographs are confusing things, jumbling up the points of compass in an unreliable manner. Joyce found that it was almost as strange as if never pictured out before her, and a great deal uglier than she had supposed. She shivered as she gazed around upon the bleakness everywhere, perhaps largely accentuated by a gray, chilly morning of early spring, with the small patches of snow, left by winter, blackened and foul. Ellen Dover, at her elbow, remarked plaintively,

"There, Miss Joyce, I knowed you'd need your sealskin such a day," to which the girl only answered, with an odd smile,

"Even a sealskin couldn't stop that shiver, Ellen; it might make it worse, indeed. Come, I think this is the way to the office. Doesn't it say something over that door at the right? Yes, there it is—come on!"

They traversed a considerable space of uneven ground crossed and recrossed by the narrow-gauge tracks upon which the sand and grit trucks ran, avoiding one or two localities where steam shot upward from the ground in a witch-like and erratic manner, with short angry hisses and chopping sounds that suggested danger, and finally stood before the door designated "OFFICE" in plain lettering. Joyce looked around at her companion with a perplexed little laugh.

"Do we knock, Ellen? How does one do at a place like this,—just walk in as it 'twere a shop, or wait till you're let in, as at a house?"

"Goodness me!" bridled Ellen, gazing at the uninviting

exterior. "Why should you be knocking and waiting when you own the whole business, I'd like to know? Just push in and tell who you be—that's what I'd do."

"Oh, I think not, Ellen—would you? I'd rather err on the safe side, seems to me. Do let's be polite, at least! Yes, I'll knock," and a timid rat-tat-tat, made by a small kid-covered knuckle, announced the first visit of the present owner of the great Early Works.

After an instant's delay the door was partly opened, and a preoccupied face, with perpendicular lines between the keen gray eyes, was thrust out impatiently, with the words,

"Well, why don't you come in? What—Oh, excuse me, ladies. Good-morning! What can I do for you?"

"Is Mr. Dalton in?" asked Joyce embarrassedly.

"Yes, I am he; please walk in. You'll have to excuse the litter here. I've been too busy to let them clean it up. Here's a chair, Miss—and here, ma'am"—calmly overturning two close beside the desk, that were heaped with papers.

Having thus seated his guests, the man stood in an inquiring attitude, surreptitiously glancing at Joyce who seemed to him almost superhumanly beautiful in that dusty place, for her pink flush and shy eyes only accentuated her charms. She found it necessary to explain the intrusion at once, but was so nervous over just the right form of self-introduction required that she rather lost her head, and stammered out,

"I—I thought I'd like to see the works and—and you"—then stopped, feeling how awkward was this beginning.

A smile flitted over his grave countenance.

　　　　　　Fannie E. Newberry

"I am before you," he said, bowing somewhat elaborately. "If looking at me can do anybody any good—"

She checked him with a somewhat imperious gesture.

"I am Joyce Lavillotte," she said, growing cool again, "and I would like to look the place over."

The sentence died into silence before an ejaculation so amazed and long-drawn it made Joyce's eyes open wide. The man looked ready to burst into laughter, yet full of respect, too. At length he broke out,

"I beg your pardon! I am so surprised. I supposed you were a man. It's your name, probably, that deceived me—and then I never thought of a girl—a young lady—caring to examine into things, and asking for statistics, and so on. Then your handwriting—it was so bold. And your methods of expression—well, I have been completely fooled!"

He stopped the voluble flow of words, which Joyce felt instinctively to be unlike himself, and gazed at her again in a forgetfulness somewhat embarrassing. Joyce was trying to think of something to say when he broke out once more, "Yes, I supposed of course you were a man, and not so very young, either. I had pictured you the moral image of your father"—he stopped an instant, then asked with a sort of regretful note in his voice—"he *was* your father?"

"Yes," said Joyce coldly. "Only I bear my mother's name for certain private reasons."

"Yes. I had thought Lavillotte was merely a middle name. We have always spoken of—of you—as young Early, here. But excuse me! I am very glad to see you, Miss Lavillotte. You wish to go over the works, you say?"

"Yes, if perfectly convenient. And I want, if possible, to go inside one or two of the houses, if I may. Could it be managed, Mr. Dalton?"

"Assuredly. Just let me announce you, and they'll be honored—"

"But wait a minute!" Joyce was gathering her wits again.

"Is the idea general here that I am a man?" smiling up into his face so blithely that his eyes reflected the light in hers.

"Why, yes, I'm afraid it is. You see we know so little of Mr.—of your father—in a personal way, and all I have said has been under that impression. I humbly beg your pardon for it, Miss Lavillotte."

"No, you needn't. I'm not sure but I shall thank you for the mistake, indeed. Let me think a minute. Yes, I believe I shall leave myself undiscovered for a time, at least. I may see things more exactly as they are in that way. But don't they know my name at all, Mr. Dalton?"

"I think not. You have only been mentioned as Early's son, I am certain. There has been no occasion to speak of the heir except to one or two, and I know the name Early was given him."

Joyce could scarcely keep from laughing outright at his tone and manner, for he could not yet conceal his sense of the unexpected, even the ludicrous, in this denouement. And if it so impressed him, might it not also make her something of a laughing-stock among her people, as she liked to call them? Would they give her credit for knowing enough to try and promote their interests in all she did? The idea of remaining incognito appealed still more strongly to her, and she

Fannie E. Newberry

said slowly,

"I don't exactly relish the role of impostor, but it might be justifiable in this case. Mr. Dalton, I want to make improvements here that shall benefit the people directly, and I don't want to begin by having them laugh at me—as you are doing."

He glanced up quickly at the reproachful tone, but catching the gleam of fun in her eye relaxed happily.

"I didn't mean to," he said contritely, "but you took me so by surprise! I am ready, now, to do whatever you wish done, and there shall be no more laughing."

"Well, then, could we not—this is Miss Dover, Mr. Dalton— couldn't we pass as acquaintances of yours, say? Don't people ever come to look the Works over?"

"Not often, but they might. And shall I invent new names for you both?" His manner was as alert as Joyce's own, now, and the perpendicular lines were nearly smoothed out between his eyes.

"No. If, as you say, my name is unknown we will not dye ourselves too deeply in deception. I think I'll remain Joyce Lavillotte, thank you! Can we start at once?"

He seemed pleased at her eagerness, but gave her handsome mourning costume a perplexed glance.

"Assuredly, only—I don't know much about such things, but aren't you pretty well dressed to go around in the worst parts? There are some dirty places, though it's clean work in the main. I know you wish to be thorough," with an approving glance, "so I mention it. You haven't any old frock that you could get at near by?"

At this instant Ellen was heard to give a little sniff and both turned their gaze upon her, Dalton's questioning, and Joyce's laughing and deprecatory.

"Did you speak, Ellen?" she asked mischievously.

"No 'm, I didn't, but I was just a-thinkin' that if you'd 'a' listened to me and wore your old Henrietta-cloth—"

"But as usual I did not listen, Ellen, and we won't scold now about unimportant matters. Lead on, Mr. Dalton; we're ready."

The man reached for his hat, closed his ledger carefully upon the pen he had been using, then opened an inner door, and stood aside to let them pass on through a short, narrow entry, from which another door led them directly into the noise and vapors of the Works.

Fannie E. Newberry

CHAPTER IV

THE WORKS AND WORKMEN

It would not be best to attempt a detailed description of the Early Glass Works, lest the subject prove so interesting we forget our story. There are few industries so fascinating to watch, or even to read about, as that of glass-blowing, and on this inspection morning Joyce had to keep reminding herself that she had come, primarily, to study the workmen and not the process, so absorbed did she frequently become in the latter.

The Early Works made a specialty of flint-glass crystal, and cut and engraved ware for domestic and ornamental use, also of the finer qualities of shades for lamps and chandeliers. As Joyce lingered again and again to watch the swift and graceful shaping of the molten substance, while airy stem or globe were blown into being by the breath of man, to be afterwards carved into exquisite designs upon the emery-wheel, or graven against the spindle, all with a dexterity that seemed simply marvelous to her ignorance, she decided in her own mind that a master at glass working was not an artisan, but an artist.

Mr. Dalton seemed amused at her child-like delight, and tried to explain all she observed in language not too technical for her comprehension. But often she became too absorbed to question, or even listen, at which times he stood silently by, watching with open admiration her fair, expressive face.

Dalton was, in a sense, a self-made man, having begun as stoker of one of the annealing furnaces when both he and the Works were young. He had climbed steadily, serving his apprenticeship in each department, and studying at a night-school, when such were in operation, until the sudden demise of Mr. Early had lifted him from the position of foreman to that of manager, by right of a thorough understanding of the business. He was a plain thoughtful-seeing man, in his thirties, who showed by his terse speech, practical manner, and business garb that he had no intention of forgetting his work-a-day life in his present elevation. Perhaps he had never so keenly felt how entirely it had been a work-a-day life until this morning.

After a time Joyce ceased to feel dazed over the dull roar of the furnaces, the flash and glow of the fiery masses of molten glass as lifted from the pots, the absorbing sight of the blowing, rolling, clipping, joining, cutting, and engraving, and the precision and silence of the white-aproned, sometimes mask-protected workmen. She could begin to notice individuals and study faces.

She stopped, finally, close by the marver of a young man— boy she called him to herself—the precision of whose workmanship was that of a machine. He was shaping a slender, long-stemmed, pitcher-like vase made in three parts, foot, body and handle, afterwards joining them in one exquisitely fine whole, after the manner of the Clichy crystal ware. He was a remarkable looking being, she thought, divided between studying his face and admiring his workmanship. Though somewhat deformed, with a curving back and high shoulders, the face that crowned this

Fannie E. Newberry

misshapen figure might have been the original of one of those intaglios of Venice, which seem to reproduce all that is refined and choice in human features. He had the broad brow, delicate, sensitive nose, curved and mobile lips, and the square, slightly cleft chin that make up an almost perfect outline. Yet the large dark eyes bore an expression of such hopelessness, such unyouthful gravity, that the whole face seemed gloomed over, as when a heavy cloud shuts out the brilliant sunshine of an August day. He did not deign so much as a glance towards the visitors, but like an automaton blew the graceful bulb, shaped it upon his marver, with a light, skilful blow detached it from his blowing-iron, received from his assistant the foot and joined the two, with a dextrous twist and turn shaped the slender handle and added that, all the time keeping his "divining-rod" (as Joyce named it to herself) turning, rolling, advancing, receding, as if it were some inspired wand, impelled to create the absolutely beautiful in form and finish. As they slowly passed on Joyce breathed out involuntarily,

"Poor boy! He seems too sad even to wish for anything."

Dalton gave her a quick, keen glance.

"You have guessed it, Miss Lavillotte. He's got where he doesn't care. He is one of our finest workmen, and a good fellow, but he is so unsocial and gloomy the other boys all shun him."

"Do you know his story?" asked Joyce with interest.

"Why, yes, I know something of him. It isn't much of a story, though," laughing a little. "We don't go much into romancing here. He had a twin brother that was as handsome as he in the face, and straight and tall into the bargain; in fact, as fine a fellow as you'll see in a century—and he shot him last year."

"Shot him?" Joyce recoiled in horror.

"Yes, accidentally of course. Their father had been a soldier in the civil war, and in some way the rifle he carried, with his name and the date scratched on the trigger-plate, was sent to the boys by a comrade after his death. Dan, there, was handling it, supposing it unloaded as usual, when it went off and shot his brother, who was leaning over him, right through the heart. That's all."

"*All!*" Joyce breathed the word with a meaning, practical George Dalton scarcely understood, and they proceeded in silence.

One other of the workers attracted the girl, as instantly, and partially distracted her thoughts from Dan. This was a girl with a peculiar face; not handsome. Joyce could only think of one descriptive word—high. Pale, with dark coloring in hair and eyes, she seemed somehow remote, lifted above the common life about her, like one living in a world of her own. She, too, seemed absorbed in her work of engraving, and did not for an instant remove her eyes from her delicate task, as she slowly turned and pressed the globe against the spindle, working out the pattern etched in the film covering its surface. But Joyce asked no questions about her as they passed on.

"Now for the homes," she said, after the long tour of the buildings was completed. "How can we gain entrance without seeming to intrude? Had we better all try to go? It will seem like a regular incursion, won't it?"

Mr. Dalton smiled.

"If you could let me out, I'd be grateful. I've a big day's work laid out on the time-books and accounts, for to-morrow's

Fannie E. Newberry

pay-day. But of course, if you need me—"

"No, no. It has been very good of you to give us so much time. If I were only an agent, now, and had something to sell—"

"'Twouldn't be a bad scheme, Miss Lavillotte, in case you really want to see them as they are. If you had some new-fangled baking dish, or a story paper, or—"

Joyce looked up with a flashing glance, and turned to Ellen, who received the notice with a sniff and a restrained smile.

"You have one, Ellen. We bought it on the train, It's full of pictures and short stories."

"Yes 'm, I've got it. You left it on the seat and I picked it up."

"And now your frugality is to be rewarded. But wouldn't it be prying, Mr. Dalton?"

"Possibly. But wouldn't it be, anyway? I gather you have some good reason for wishing to see these people at home."

"I have. I want to know just how and where to help them best, but I hate to act in an underhanded way. And yet, if the paper would serve to give me entrance I'd try not to prevaricate in the least."

"I think you may be trusted, Miss Lavillotte."

"Ellen, will you stay here in the office while I try it alone?"

"If you tell me to I s'pose I must, but I think it's a wild-goose chase anyhow," was the disapproving answer. "I can tell you what you'll find well enough," sniffing disgustedly, "and that is babies, bad smells, dirt, and scolding. I've been there afore!"

Joyce laughed gaily.

"Give me the story paper, Ellen. I'm going to find all those things, surely, but more—much more, as you'll see in time," and, snatching the sheet from her maid's reluctant hand, she was off with a merry look back at the two, who watched her till she had rounded the corner of the great building and disappeared.

"It's a queer streak!" muttered Dalton, as he turned back into the little office room, which had never looked so dim and dingy before. "For a girl that's rich and handsome—"

"Don't see what there is so queer in being good!" returned Ellen belligerently. "Just 'cause she's got a heart and sense beyond her years folks calls her a freak. Of course it cuts, but she only laughs and goes on just the same's ever. I get so mad, sometimes, I'd like to stomp on 'em, but she just looks at me smiling brave-like, with her lips twitching a bit, and says, 'Never mind so long's we're surely right,' and then I can't say a word."

Dalton looked at her reflectively. He was not used to women, and it struck him, once or twice, that this elderly companion would have liked to dictate to her young mistress, had the latter allowed it. So, not feeling quite sure of his ground, he remarked vaguely,

"I suppose a girl like that would be naturally wilful—having everything heart could wish. But—"

"Well then, I'll let you know she isn't," snapped Miss Dover. "Wilful indeed!" and seating herself with resentful suddenness she glared at him till he was glad to bury himself in his books, and try to forget the excitements of the morning in figures.

CHAPTER V

AMONG THE COTTAGES

Joyce, laughing to herself, tripped across the ground occupied by the works, and, after a hurried glance along the first row of cottages, selected one at random and making straight for it, knocked with some trepidation, but no delay. She heard herself announced inside by a childish voice in descriptive fashion—"Say, ma, it's a girl in swell clothes—hurry!" and began to question if she were too well dressed, even in her plain black garb, for her part. Certainly there was an air about her not common to the traveling agency people, but whether it were entirely due to her garments may be doubted.

After considerable scurrying about inside, plainly distinguished through the thin planking, the door was gingerly opened a few inches and a touzled head appeared in the slit.

"Good-morning, 'm," spoke the head with an inquiring accent, which plainly meant, "And what do you want?"

Joyce partly ignored the woman and her brusquerie, for the pretty curly pate of a baby clinging to her skirts, and her ready smile was for him, as she said,

Fannie E. Newberry

"What a bright-eyed baby! May I come in for a minute and talk to you?"

The mother thawed to that, and the door fell wide apart. "Why, yes, come in, come in! I'm washing to-day, but there's no great hurry's I knows on. Sit there, won't ye? It's more comfor'ble."

Quite willing to be "more comfor'ble," if at no one's expense, Joyce sank into the old cane rocker, still beaming upon the baby, who shyly courted her from amid the damp folds of his mother's skirts.

"He's pretty smart for 'leven months," affirmed the latter, lifting him to her knee, and dropping into the wooden chair opposite with a sense of utter relaxation that struck the caller as being the next thing to unconscious grace, even in that lank, slatternly figure. "He can go clear 'round the room by takin' hold o' things. I guess you like babies, 'm?"

"I like some babies—and yours is a beauty; large, too. I had thought him much older."

"Yes, he's as big as I care to lug—that's certain! Dorey, go and stir down the clo'es in the boilin' suds, and be quick about it, too! Don't ye know better'n to stand starin' at folks like a sick cat?" This, to a little girl, presumably the herald of Joyce's approach, who had been peeping in through the crack of a rear door.

Joyce, dreading a storm, asked politely,

"You have two children, have you?"

The woman laughed with something of a bitter cadence. "Oh yes, and seven more atop o' them. There's two between baby and Dorey, and five older. My three oldest is in the Works, and Rache is about the best hand they've got, if I do say it. Rache earns good wages, I tell ye—better'n the boys. But then, what with tobacco and beer, and beauin' the girls around to dances and shows, and all, you can't expect a fellow to have much left for his own folks. And my other two gals is workin' out in town. Dorey, stop jouncin' them hot clo'es up an' down in the suds! You'll git scalt with 'em yit."

"Do any of your children go to school?" asked the caller, quickly.

The woman laughed shortly.

"Where'd they go? There ain't no schools around here, and we ain't wanting any, either, since our time with that one last year. 'Twas a reg'lar sell! The gal what kep' it asked a nickel a week for every young 'un, and left us right in the middle of a term, 'cause she said it didn't pay. Stuck-up thing she was, too! Couldn't see nothin' lower'n the top of her own head, I couldn't abide her! No, if you're thinkin' of gettin' up any of them kinter-gardens you might as well give it up," eying Joyce suspiciously. "We don't want 'em."

"But would you object to a free public school?" asked Joyce with a patient air.

"Oh, I don't know's I should object," tolerantly. "Rache, she's a great hand to read, and she takes in a magerzine, too, but I never could see the sense o' spendin' time and money that way. If she marries she'll hev to come down to scrubbin' and cookin', and tendin' baby, same's her ma; and if she's an old maid, why, there's the Works, or goin' out to housework, and either way I don't see just where an eddication comes in."

"It might help her to some easier employment," suggested

Joyce, but rather faintly, for the woman's airy loquacity disconcerted her.

"It might, an' then it mightn't. I've seen girls as got above their business come down a good deal lower than what they started from, and I say, let well enough alone. There's lots of born ladies that ain't no softer spoken than my girl Rache, and she's good to me and the young 'uns. I don't want anybody spoilin' my fam'ly by these highfalutin' notions."

The woman assumed a Cornelia expression that almost daunted poor Joyce, who was half a coward at heart, anyhow, so she meekly rose to go.

"I won't delay you from your washing any longer; good-by," she said, nodding at the baby, who showed pearly teeth in return; and she passed out, nor realized until later that she had not posed as a canvasser here, unless in an educational sense.

She felt just a trifle discouraged by the unflinching attitude of this Spartan mother, and was proportionately surprised when, obeying a call to enter at the next door, she stepped into a bright, tastefully furnished apartment with flowers in the window and magazines on the table. Near by, in a large invalid chair reclined a girl—nay, a woman, as Joyce decided after the second look, though a small creature— busily embroidering upon a little frame, while on a small, detachable table, now screwed to the arm of her chair, was a bright array of silks, and beside them a half-open book, with a pencil slid between its leaves. She gave Joyce an inquiring glance, and waited for her to speak. The latter flushed a little, scarcely knowing how to introduce herself, but a second look towards the magazines touched up her memory, and she began graciously,

"I see you are a reader. I wonder if you would care for the paper I have here," and she handed it over for inspection.

"Ah, I cannot tell if 'tis so; pray be seated ma'amselle. Yes, I like mooch those peectures and those patterns. They do help in my work." Her accent was distinctly foreign, yet every word was so plainly enunciated that it was easy to understand her. "You do sell this?" she asked.

Joyce was nonplussed, but caught at her waning wits enough to answer,

"Not this copy. It is only for you to look at."

"Ah yes,"—quickly, with a merry smile, "It ees a sahmple, eh?"

"Yes, a sample copy, but if you think you could use it in your work I will see that you have it every month."

"And the expense of it?" She looked up apprehensively. "That, too, must be considered."

"Surely. You see it says ten cents a number, or one dollar a year. But I think I might furnish you a sample copy free, if you would speak a good word for it among your neighbors. Not to trouble yourself any, of course."

"That is most kind, and I could do it. The girls do coom in and listen as I read, by times. It is a great deal that books do for one like me, ma'amselle. They are my friends, my coomfort. They, and my vork."

"I can well believe it. And what beautiful work you do! Doesn't it tire you while in that reclining position? You look so delicate."

"But I am so mooch bettare—quite near to well once more. I do this, while my sister, she work in the glass-house. She is all well and strong—my sister."

"That is good! And you live here alone together?"

"Yes, we do. We come across from Havre together—we, the two—and we think we will make a fortune, now we have lost our parents, and have no big strong brother. And then it is I that must get sick, and when the fevaer do go after the long weeks, it takes with it all my strength, and so I cannot yet walk."

"Poor little woman! But you have such a pretty room—how kind your sister must be."

"My Babette? Ah, she is so bright, so gay. She will not let me say that we have been onlooky—oh no! She say, 'You here, I here, nevare mind any other thing.' So she coomfort me."

"And do you send this beautiful embroidery into the city?"

"Yes, I do. To an eschange for womans. I have teeket and that make me one member."

"I see; 'tis an excellent plan. But who keeps house for you?"

"Oh, that is an easy thing. I do skin off the potatoes and schop up the meat for the hash, and Babette, she do sweep with the broom and set out the table. And while we work she can tell me all there is going about outside, and I can tell how mooch bettare I am doing this day—do not you see?"

"I see you must be very happy together! But do you stay alone all day! And what if you need something, meanwhile?"

she laughed.

"See?" with a comprehensive sweep of the hands, "I have everything. But for fear I do get sick, see this?"

She put out her hand to a rope dangling along the wall close beside her. "When I pull hard once Lucie, in the next house, knows that I would like to see her, but it is not bad; when I pull twice then she must indeed run quick, for I need her. She is so good, little Lucie!"

By her motions Joyce knew she was speaking of the house upon the opposite side from that where she herself had just called. So, feeling she must economize her time, and anxious to learn all she could, she asked at once,

"Who is this Lucy? Please tell me about her."

There was a way with Joyce that made people like to confide in her. She was so bright and pretty, so interested, and so free from guile, that hearts opened to her as blossoms to the sun. One could not long be reserved in her presence. The invalid smiled upon her and chatted on in her odd English, telling of the children next door lately left motherless, where the oldest girl, Lucy, aged sixteen, was bravely keeping house for father, and looking after two younger girls, a baby boy, just learning to toddle alone and a younger baby of a few months. It was evident a great friendship existed between this little Frenchwoman and the maiden, and that there was mutual helpfulness in their intercourse, Lucy bringing youthful cheer and strength to exchange for thoughtful lessons in some of the finer ways of living, not common here.

"I hope her father is very good to her!" cried Joyce, becoming at once a partisan of the plucky child, upon whom the other was showering encomiums. "Only sixteen, and doing all that! Is he a fine workman? Does he earn much?"

"Yes, when he do work." The embroiderer bent over her frame with renewed diligence, and shut her lips together in a determined way.

"I understand," said Joyce quickly, with a little sigh; "he isn't quite steady?"

"I would nevare say ill of him. He mean well—oh, yes! But he do not know when it is time to leave off. He take one drink, that make him talk loud and laugh; he take two, that make him swear bad worts and knock round the furniture; he take t'ree, that make him come home and beat thos poor leetle girls till it make your heart sore! And poor Lucie will try so hard, and then he will be so oogly—but I should not so speak to a strangare."

"Don't let that trouble you; it shall go no further. I will try and see this Lucy, soon. What is her other name?"

"It is Hapgood, ma'amselle. I pray you to forge: I have ill spoke of a man who means to be kind, but so troubled he must try somehow to forget his cares. Many men are like that. And of a truth there is no place to go for rest. In the small house the children do cry and quarrel, and tired Lucie will scold at times, and he does come home so weary, himself. If all is not to please him he snatches his hat and goes rushing away—but where? The only place that makes welcome is the saloon—you know it."

"Yes, yes, I do know. And the poor children, too! They ought to have places where they can be jolly and make a noise besides in these barren streets. Tell me, Mrs.—"

"I am not that," laughing merrily, "I am Marie Sauzay, and

my sister, she is Babette, though everybody makes it Bab for short, and she likes the little name."

"I can imagine it is like her—short and sweet. Well, Ma'amselle Marie, tell me this. Is there no public hall here— no place of meeting where the people may go for music, or pleasure. Don't you have any amusements?"

"Amusements!" Marie laughed outright. "And who would care to amuse us, who have to work? No, no, that is not to be thought of. That Mr. Early, who is the high boss, he would laugh at such a question. What have we to do with amusements?"

Joyce winced at what seemed to her a direct slur upon her father's memory, but knew it was just. She could fairly hear him laugh as Marie spoke, sitting back in an easy attitude, perhaps mixing a julep and cackling amusedly in that peculiar voice that was curiously like a scolding woman's. How often she had heard him say, "Don't try to mix business and philanthropy, my dear. It won't work. As well hope to combine oil and water. You would only spoil the one and make a mess of the other. The working-classes are best off when let quite alone. If you don't want them to override you, be careful to keep them well down. Once let them see you mean to give them any leeway, and they are only content with a revolution. You can give away as much as you like in charity, but just leave me to manage the Works, if you please."

She sighed once more, and rose to her feet.

"Thank you for your courtesy," she said, happening to remember her ostensible errand. "I shall send you the paper soon, and may some day see you again. Good-by!"

She passed out, smiling back at the little woman until she

Fannie E. Newberry

had softly closed the door, then her young face relapsed into grave thoughtfulness.

"How large and formidable evil seems when one sets out to battle with it!" she murmured. "I wonder, is it really so powerful, or does it diminish on a closer view, like all things seen through a mist? Can I ever accomplish what I have determined upon? Well, at least I can die trying, as Leon used to say."

She smiled, and a soft look crept over her face though she had set her little teeth in stubborn fashion. She bent her head as if in retrospect, and walked some distance, apparently forgetful of her purpose, before she finally selected another door at random, and sought admittance.

CHAPTER VI

FRESH GLIMPSES

It was high noon when Joyce came quickly into the office, her face pale and set, and a strange expression in her eyes.

"Mr. Dalton," she said, without any preliminaries, "did you know that Gus Peters has been frightfully burned with some of the molten glass, this morning, and has no one to take care of him? His hands and arms are so bad he is perfectly helpless, and there's no one in the house but a stupid child that is too frightened to do anything but stare. Isn't there a doctor here, or somebody? Ellen, you and I must attend to him, if there isn't. He is suffering awfully!"

"That Gus Peters!" said the manager with a disgusted accent. "He always was an awkward lout. Of course there's a doctor—why didn't he send for him?"

"Send! Haven't I told you there was nobody to wait upon him? How could he send, mad with pain as he is, and that child scared out of all the wits it ever had? And no telephone, nor even an errand-boy anywhere. How can I get the doctor? Which way shall I go? Don't you appreciate the fact that something must be *done*!"

Fannie E. Newberry

She was talking so fast and excitedly the man could only stand and gaze at her, but spurred by her impatient gesture he broke out beseechingly:

"Please wait a minute, and I'll send a boy. But you needn't worry so! These accidents are happening—that is, often happen. They get used to them. It's because Gus is new at the business. Excuse me a moment."

He disappeared through the door into the work-room, and Joyce tramped up and down the office as if caged, now stopping to look out of the dingy windows, now leaning over the desk as if to examine the papers upon it, but with a face set in such troubled lines it was obvious she saw nothing. Ellen looked on with an unflinching expression. She was evidently used to these moods, and did not favor them, but wisely held her peace.

Presently Mr. Dalton returned, looking a bit anxious and grim.

"They've gone for Dr. Browne and he'll see to Gus all right. But you look very tired. Won't you go home with me to dinner? I have 'phoned my aunt to—"

"'Phoned? Why, I thought—I don't see—"

He smiled indulgently.

"Oh, it's an individual affair I had put up. I found it inconvenient not to have some method of communication as we are nearly ten minutes' walk apart."

"Ah yes, it is inconvenient—especially in cases of real need, such as dinner, for instance. Thank you, but I think—"

Ellen, who had risen at Mr. Dalton's first word of dinner, now advanced with alacrity.

"I hope we can go somewheres," she exclaimed with asperity, "for I'm all one cramp setting still so long. And you know you'll have a headache if you don't eat something, Miss Joyce; you allays do."

The latter laughed impatiently.

"Oh, my headaches! You feel them more than I do, Ellen. However—well, yes, Mr. Dalton, thank you, we will be very glad to accompany you. Now tell me, please, where is there some good, kind man or woman to go and nurse that boy?"

"You mean Gus? Oh, really, Miss Lavillotte, he couldn't pay anybody if you sent them. The neighbors will look after him. They're kind in such cases. Let's see"—bowing his guests out of the door and locking it behind him—"Gus keeps bachelor's hall with two or three of the other boys, doesn't he? Oh, they'll see to him—don't you worry! There'll be a crowd to wait on him, now it's nooning hour. They are positively happy when there's an accident to stir them up. It breaks the monotony. This way, please, it's a bit rougher than by the street, but cuts off half a block. Perhaps, though, you'd rather—"

"No, no, this way's all right. Mr. Dalton," sternly, "were you ever badly burned?"

The man turned with a sharp movement, and looked at her. "Why I—I don't know that I ever was. Not seriously, you know."

"Well, *I* have been."

Fannie E. Newberry

Joyce pushed up the sleeve of her jacket and drew down her glove with a quick motion, full of repressed intensity. He had just a glimpse of a red scar on the white flesh when, with as sudden a motion and a rosy flush, she dropped her arm and let the sleeve fall over her wrist, then added more gently,

"One knows how it hurts when one has suffered oneself. I was only eight years old, but I have never forgotten the day I tripped and fell against a red-hot stove—and I had the tenderest and most constant care, too."

Had Joyce been looking at her companion's face she would no doubt have been made furious by its expression. If ever a laugh struggled in a man's eyes, trying to break bounds, it struggled now in George Dalton's gray orbs! After an instant, which Joyce fondly imagined was given to silent sympathy, he said gently,

"Burns are serious things, I know. Miss Lavillotte, I began stroking for the furnaces here when I was eight years old. I think"—looking off in an impersonal manner, as if reckoning a problem,—"that from that time on to fourteen, at least, I was never without burns on face, hands or arms. Probably I grew used to them."

Joyce looked up quickly. He was quite serious now, and seemed almost to have forgotten the subject up between them. Joyce felt suddenly very young, and she devoutly wished she had never consented to this detestable visit with her manager. Then pride came to her aid, and she asked deliberately, with an intrepid air,

"I doubt if people ever really get used to pain. Do you think the doctor will be through with that boy in half an hour?"

"Possibly. Of course I don't know the extent of his injuries."

"Let us hurry then," doubling her pace. "I shall have none too much time before the 2.39 train, and we must take that, as I have an engagement in the city. Ellen, am I tiring you?"

The maid smiled grimly. She understood this as an overture for peace, knowing her young mistress was never so thoughtful and conciliatory as just after being most unreasonable and peremptory. She rightly conjectured that the girl was already ashamed of her sharpness, and wished to make amends in some way. Mr. Dalton's slower comprehension of womankind was bewildered by these rapid changes. Having inwardly decided, in spite of Ellen's favorable testimony, that here was a young lady who had been allowed her own way more than was good for her, he was left stranded on the shore of his own conjectures by her present tone. He had mentally dubbed her a sort of princess, determined to have her say in everything; now she seemed a child eager to be led by any one. But Ellen was answering with fine sarcasm.

"I might walk faster, too, if I hadn't got 'most paralyzed on them wooden chairs. But never mind! Keep right on—I guess I can manage to get there, if I try hard."

Fortunately for her legs and temper, they stopped presently before a rather ornate cottage, with several peaks and a turret, which was set down in the midst of a square lawn that looked unnaturally green to Joyce in comparison with the bareness all about it. Grass, except in long scraggy tufts here and there, or in sparse blades in some odd fence corner, was not prevalent at the Works. Joyce liked all that was trim and beautiful, but just now this house and lawn, so new and snug and smiling, jarred upon her like a discordant note. What business had he to live where fresh paint and large windows and broad verandas should mock at the poverty and squalor of all the other houses? She felt it almost as a personal insult.

Fannie E. Newberry

Mr. Dalton, to whom a neat home of his own was still a novelty, was a trifle hurt by her lack of enthusiasm. He had really looked for a girlish "Oh, how pretty!" and somewhat resented Miss Lavillotte's quiet way of saying,

"I see you have been able to make yourself comfortable, even in this forbidding spot, Mr. Dalton."

But he answered cheerfully,

"Oh, yes, yes. It seems good to have a home after so many years of fifth-rate boarding houses. And the best of it is, my good aunt, who has had a hard time breasting the world, enjoys it even more than I."

The girl did not speak at once. She was distinctly ashamed of herself. Then she broke out quickly:

"I see. It was most good of you. I am hasty as an ill-tempered child in my judgments! Mr. Dalton"—she stopped before the neat iron gate in the low fence, which he was holding open for her to pass through, and barring the way, said rapidly, "as we will have to work together in all that is done here, I may as well say at once—I am often quick, irascible, unkind. I want things to move at once, and when they don't it makes me cross. It isn't because I—I have money, though—you mustn't think it. I am not such a cad! It's just my nature, that's all. I can't help it, and it cuts me up when I come to my senses more than it possibly can anybody else. There! Shall we be friends and co-workers, or not?"

She held out her small gloved hand, and as he warmly clasped it, a flush that was so strange to his bronzed cheek it fairly colored for its own temerity, made his face foolishly warm. He laughed out like a boy.

"Why, you are the boss, of course," he said with a ring of delight in his voice. "I shall do exactly what you tell me to—how could I help it?"

"No, you must help it," gravely. "I really am young and inexperienced, as Mr. Barrington says. But these ideas are better than I—they really are! When you come to see what I mean, and what I want to do, you will approve, I am sure."

She was so eager for this approval that he felt positively dazed by the situation. He could not follow such spiral flights, such swoopings and dartings of mood. He could only look on and be ready to her hand the instant she might alight beside him. So he only murmured, "Depend upon me for any assistance whatever!" thinking meanwhile, with a sense of relief, "Aunt Margaret will understand her; she's a woman."

They had barely stepped within the modern hall when a tall figure advanced between the heavy portieres at one side to meet them. Mrs. Margaret Phelps was rather finely formed, but had no other beauty except a heavy head of silvery white hair. Yet Joyce thought, for a homely woman she was the best-looking one she had ever seen! There was sense and kindness in her face, as well as a certain self-respect, which drew out answering respect to meet it. She acknowledged her nephew's introduction with that embarrassed stiffness common to those unused to social forms, but the grasp of her large hand was warm and consoling, and her voice had a hearty genuineness, as she remarked,

"My nephew, George, says you've been looking at the Works. It isn't many young ladies would care to come so far outside of the city just to see them. They wouldn't think it worth while."

Joyce exchanged a quick glance with Dalton and knew her

identity had not been divulged, so answered easily,

"Oh, don't you think so? It was like an enchanted land to me this morning! It was all so far beyond me I could only look on and wonder; but to watch a vase grow into perfect form at a breath was a real marvel of creation."

"Well, yes, I guess it's so. I always feel that way, too, when I see an engine. It seems such a grand thing that anybody could get the parts all fitted together, and then dare to start it when it was done. You can understand how folks may learn figures and poetry, and even engineering—but to go back and make the things they have to learn about; that beats me!"

Joyce laughed with her, while Mrs. Phelps took her wraps, then relinquished them to Ellen, who stood by like a sentinel awaiting their movements. She seemed to find the presence of the maid somewhat embarrassing, and followed her laden figure into the hall, to whisper,

"Say, I've got a real nice lady sewing for me. Wouldn't you like to get acquainted with her?"

"Don't know as I mind," returned Ellen, and followed into the next room. During the space his aunt was absent, Dalton took up the conversation where it had dropped.

"We always think things are hardest to do that are out of our sphere, don't we? I suppose, now, you and Aunt Margaret could both understand making a dress, couldn't you?"

"Oh yes, even though I could not do it," laughed Joyce.

"Well, and I can imagine building the engine, but as for the frock"—he looked at her and made a gesture of impotence— "I should never even attempt it, though I were to lose my head for not trying. In the first place," glancing from the trim, smooth, tailor-made black gown of his guest to the home-cut skirt and shirt-waist of his aunt, just entering, and dimly discerning the difference, "I never thought of it before, but I cannot even conceive how you get into and out of the things. I suppose you do, for I see you women in different ones at times, but my thought would be that they must grow upon you"—he was looking at Joyce—"as the calyx around a blossom. It all seems merged into you, somehow. I never felt it so before."

Mrs. Phelps laughed with hearty enjoyment.

"It's the cut of it, George! You never felt that way looking at me, or—or Rachel Hemphill, say—did you?"

"Why no; it seems a new sensation," laughing half shame-facedly. "But it may be just because the talk called it up. Isn't dinner ready—well, I thought it was time."

A somewhat strident-sounding bell announced it, and the three passed directly into the next room, furnished so conventionally there was absolutely nothing upon which to let the eyes rest in surprise, or pleasure. But it was painfully neat and regular, and both aunt and nephew were secretly satisfied that it must impress even this young heiress as a perfectly proper dining-room. And it did.

Ellen and the "nice lady," who had been sewing for Mrs. Phelps, joined them at once, and the talk languished as each was called upon to help the other in a wearisome round of small dishes, which it seemed to Joyce was like the stage processions that simply go out at one side to come in at the other. But when she tasted of these she no longer begrudged their number. They were each deliciously palatable, having a taste so new to her hotel-sated palate that she could almost

Fannie E. Newberry

have smacked her lips over them in her enjoyment. She had a healthy girlish appetite and the morning had been long. She positively wanted to pass back one or two of the saucers for refilling, but was ashamed of her greediness. Had she known that it would have rejoiced Mrs. Phelps for days to be thus honored by real appreciation of the dainties she had herself prepared, she certainly would have done so. Even Ellen forgot to sniff, and all set to with a vigor that rather precluded conversation.

She thought about it afterwards, as she sat in the train, moving rapidly citywards, and wondered why there had been such positive pleasure in the mere taste of food. She had sat and minced over rich dishes day after day, and never felt that exquisite sense of wholesomeness and recuperation.

She turned to Ellen.

"Did you ever eat such nice things before? What made them so good, anyhow?"

Ellen smiled with unusual relaxation.

"They was nice, wa'n't they? Well, I'll tell you what my mother used to say, and she was the best cook in Eaton county, by all odds. Them things made me think of her to-day. She used to say that 'twas with cooking just like 'twas with church work, or anything else. You'd got to put heart into it, as well as muscle. She said these hired cooks just put in muscle and skill, and they stopped there. But when a mother was cooking for her own fam'ly she put in them, and heart besides, and that was why men was allays telling about their mother's cooking. That was what she said, and I guess she come as near to it as most folks."

"I guess she did," assented Joyce. "Well, if I can put into my work the same quality Mrs. Phelps puts into her cooking I shall make a success of it; won't I, Ellen?"

"Don't ask me!" was the quick response, as the maid drew herself up into the austere lines she affected. "You must remember hearts don't amount to much till they've been hammered out by hard knocks. You'll do your best, I presume, but what can a young thing like you understand? However, they's one thing"—

"Well, what's that?" as Ellen paused abruptly.

"Oh nothing. I was just thinking you could make anybody do anything you want 'em to, and that goes a good way. Well, well, I s'pose there is *some* advantage in being young!"

CHAPTER VII

THE HAPGOODS AND NATE

The spring was backward that year, and on its first evening of real softness and beauty the houses of Littleton seemed turned wrong-side-out, like a stocking-bag, upon the streets. Every door-step had its occupants, every fence rail its leaning groups (though fences were scarce in Littleton), and the left-overs gathered in and around the saloon, familiarly known as Lon's. Among the loungers on its broad, unroofed platform, sat two men, tilted back in wooden armchairs, talking in that slow, desultory fashion common among those who use hands more than tongues in their battle with life.

"Yes," drawled one, as he cut off a generous slice from the cake of fine-cut in his hands, "yes, I'm not saying but the town'll look better when it's done, but what's it being done for? That's what I want to know. 'Twon't make the plant any more valuable, will it?"

"It orter," was the response as the other knocked the ashes from his black pipe, blew through its stem, and proceeded to fill it from a dirty little bag drawn from his ragged coat pocket. "Good houses is better'n shanties, ain't they?"

"Of course they're better, but that's just it. We can't none of us pay any more rent than we're payin' now; so what'll he do about it?"

"Who?"

"The new man that owns it—young Early, ain't it?"

"Oh, the son; yes. It's just half way possible he thinks we ought to have something better'n pig-styes to live in!"

"Well, he isn't any Early then! I've see the old man, and I know. Straight's a glass rod, and not caring shucks for anything but his money. He'd grind a feller down to biled-tater parings, if he could."

It was Lucy's father just speaking, and his name of William Hapgood had been shortened to Bill among the villagers, who seemed to have little use for family cognomens where family pride was not a failing. He was a small man with a rasping voice and sharp nose, while the bristling growth about his chin was red and his hair brown. All this denoted temper, but not the deep and lasting kind; rather the flash-in-the-pan sort, common enough among shrewish women, and only common in men of this type. Just now his tone was bitter.

"Well, it's a change for the better anyhow, Bill," said the other, who was large, dark, stolid, and kindly. "They've shortened our hours, and allowed the shillin' a week extry. That's something."

"Oh, everything's something. I hain't seen no call to go down on my marrer-bones yet, though. You allays did slop over at nothing, Nate."

"Oh, but what's the use o' bein' so everlastingly cranky and onreasonable?"

Fannie E. Newberry

"I ain't onreasonable. I say it's you're that, when you're so pleased with the least thing. See here! Did you ever see a big boss that would go halvers with his men in flush times, and of his own notion pay 'em extry? No, you never did. But when the fires are mostly cut, oh! then we must live on half wages and be thunderin' thankful to git that. I say there ain't one o' them that cares a copper cent for one of us, 'cept just for what he can git outen us. I'm blessed if I believe they even think of us as men at all—just lump us off with the machinery, like. One man, one blowpipe, one marver—and the man least 'count of all."

The other chuckled softly, then waved his hand towards a group of shapely cottages off at the right.

"When you get into one o' them new houses, with a piazzer acrost the front, and plenty of windows, and a grass plot, and see Lucy washin' dishes at the little white sink with the hot and cold water runnin' free out of silver fassets, and know you don't have to tote your drinkin'-water a block, and ketch what rain-water you can in a bar'l, you won't feel so gritty, Bill!"

The other smiled somewhat sheepishly, pleased in spite of himself at the picture, but rallied to the challenge with—

"But what's it all *for*? That's what gets me. I can't and won't pay no more rent, and that's settled."

"Don't be allays looking fur traps, Bill."

"And don't you be walkin' into 'em open-eyed, Nate. No sir, you mark me! We ain't got to heaven yet, and in this world o' woe folks don't go and spend a big lot o' money just to make it easier fur the folks that's under 'em—'tisn't nater."

"It mayn't be your nater, nor mine, but it may be some folkses. Well, argy as you may, the place don't look the same, now does it? D'ye mind the houses they've finished off? Well they're leveling off the yards around 'em, and seedin' 'em to grass. Fact! I see it myself. And 'nother thing. They're filling up that old flat-iron place, where we used to cart rubbish to, and hauling trees to set out as they get it leveled down. If 'twa'n't perfectly ridiculous I'd say 'twas to be a park—just imagine a *park*!"

Both laughed gruffly, while a loiterer or two, just passing in or out the swing doors, who had stopped to listen, joined in.

"The thing 't really is so," observed one of these with his hand on the door, "is that they're a-goin' to have a church. It's so, Bill! Ground was broke for it to-day, and I've seen the plan, and who do you think's goin' to boss the job?"

"Who? Oh, some big architec' from town, of course," sneered Hapgood.

"Now, that's where you're off the track. It's Gus Peters."

"What? Gus Peters!"

Both men looked up, startled into real interest.

"How did it happen?" asked Nate.

"Don't know. It seems he's been studyin' the business, evenings and all. He's allays mooning over plans and drawings; and so they've give the job to him."

"Well, I never!" cried Hapgood. "That awk'ard—why, he can't finish off a glass rod without break-in' it, or burning himself!"

"No, he's no blower!" laughed the other. "Nary kind, I reckon. But they do say he's great on drawing plans. I'm glad there's something he can do, and I guess it was a lucky day for him when he burnt his arms so bad. We thought he'd have to go on the county, sure, with his hands so helpless, but he seems to 've got along first-rate."

"Did he have an accident policy?"

"Don't know. Never heard of none. They say some relation or other's been keepin' him in cash. Have a drink, Bill?"

"Well, don't care if I do. It's gettin' thirsty weather these warm days."

Nate Tierney, the dark man, looked after him and chuckled again.

"It most generally is thirsty weather for Bill," he ruminated alone as the men crowded within. "Guess I'll go along and take a look at Lucy and the babies. Kinder seems to me if I had a lot o' nice little gals like that I wouldn't git thirsty quite so often—but I don't know. The stuff's powerful comfortin' when you git tired of rememberin'—I've noticed that."

He strolled slowly down the lane-like street between the rows of houses, like peas in a pod for sameness, and stopped, with a smile on his honest face, as a little girl burst suddenly from the door of one and, closely pursued by another, just a step higher, ran shrieking with laughing fright right into his outstretched arms.

"There! I've caught you now," he cried, then called to the pursuer. "What you up to, Rufie, chasing Tilly so? Do you want to scare her into an idjit?"

Tilly, nestling in happy defiance within the shelter of his strong arm, tried to tell her woes, while Rufie dancing hotly about outside, declared in even shriller tones that Tilly deserved a slap and should get it, adding invitations to the younger girl to come out and see if she wouldn't, which were of doubtful persuasiveness. At this moment Lucy appeared in the doorway, the little baby in her arms and a larger one clinging to her skirts, to look anxiously and angrily after her younger sisters.

"I've got 'em safe, Lucy," called Nate, restraining his laughing captive and grasping at the other girl, "I'll bring in the pris'ners—don't you worry! Now, girls, be good, can't ye? What did Tilly do, Rufie, that makes you so fierce after her?"

"Stole my ribbon, the little—"

"Eh, eh! Stole is a big word for young lips," interrupted the man, while the accused protested,

"I didn't neither! I was just lookin' at it to see if 'twould match my new dress a lady guv me."

"Oh, looking!" was Rufie's sneering rejoinder. "Where is it now? Didn't I see you tuck it in your pocket, you thief o' the—"

"Sh—h! That's not nice talk for a pretty gal like you, Rufie. Don't call names like a hoodlum. Where's the ribbon, Tilly?"

"There, you old stingy!" bringing it forth with a flirt, to slap it across her sister's face, at which the later snatched it eagerly with a few choice epithets, which flowed as easily from her young lips as if she had been ages old in sin.

Fannie E. Newberry

Nate looked from one to the other, and the amused smile died out of his face.

"I don't like you when you're that way, girls," he said in a hopeless tone. "See how you worry sister!" for Lucy was calling fretfully,

"I do wish you two could be still one second! Tommy was asleep, and baby almost, when you began screeching like a fire engine and racing and slamming through the house— where's pa, Nate?"

"Pa? Oh, he—he's around uptown some'ers."

"I s'pose 'some'ers' means up to Lon's, as usual," snapped the girl bitterly. "He might better live there and be done with it."

She was a slight creature, too pale and worn for even the natural prettiness of youth, but her large, lovely eyes suggested that in a more fortunate environment she might have been described as beautiful, by that stretch of imagination which chroniclers of the great are allowed. Many a so-called beauty of high caste has shown less natural endowment than did poor Lucy, but dragging care had wiped out the life and sparkle until, no one thought of her as attractive, even—only pathetic.

The man let go of the squabbling children to lift the fretting baby from her weary arms, and followed her into the unkempt room, which made almost the sole scene in her onerous life.

"You ain't got your dishes done yet, either; have you, child?" he asked in sympathizing tones. "Well, well, I'll keep the youngsters while you red things up. Here, girls, you come now and help sister, while I 'tend baby, and we'll have things comfortable in a jiffy. Let's all try and be good together."

The admonition proved effectual. Soon the girls were quietly at work, and the little baby's startled eyes closed beneath the influence of the gentle lullaby crooned by this rough-looking man, from whom some dainty women might have shrunk in fear, had they met him on the public street. When the little one was safely deposited in his wooden cradle, the other baby, scarce two years older, being consigned to an uncomfortable nest between restless Rufie and Tilly, in a bed scarcely wide enough for them, the tired oldest sister dropped down on the door-step near kind old Nate, who sat tilted back against the house wall, the legs of his wooden chair boring deep holes in the sandy soil.

"You're pretty tired, ain't ye?" he asked with strong sympathy. "It do sorter seem as if you had more'n your share sometimes, Lucy—it do, certain sure!"

"I'd just give up if 'twa'n't for you and Marry," she returned wearily, crouching in a forlorn heap, with elbows on knees and chin in palms. "It's hard enough for women that's got their own young ones, and can mind 'em and make 'em mind. I can't do nothing with ours, and when I go to pa he just gets cross and lights out. And then he comes home—well, you know how. He hit me with a stick, last night."

Nate's strong teeth came together with a click.

"He did? The old—" His sentence ended in a mutter.

"Oh, you can curse him"—she laughed drearily—"but what good does it do? It don't take the ache out o' that welt on my arm and back any. The skin's broke and it smarts."

She began to cry in a slow, patient way.

Fannie E. Newberry

"It's queer I don't get used to it," she said presently, for Nate had not tried to answer, but was puffing like a locomotive over wet rails at his stub of a pipe. "I ought to by this time, but I don't. I s'pose it's because when pa's good he's real good, and so kind it makes it hurt all the more when he's off. Oh dear!" She gave a long sigh, pitifully unyouthful in its depth of misery. "I was 'most glad when ma got through with it all, and could rest and look so sort of peaceful in her coffin. But I dunno. She kept more offen me than I knew of, I guess, and it's growin' worse all the time."

Nate started up, letting his chair fall back with such force as to threaten total extinction to its legs.

"It's a sin and shame, and I know it!" he said in his deepest voice. "But you keep up your courage, Lucy. When things 'gets to the bottom they're bound to go up again, for they never stand still."

He stood up and knocked his pipe clean against the wooden chair seat with vigorous thumps that seemed to relieve him, and started towards the street.

"Where you going?" asked Lucy remonstrantly. "I didn't mean to nag at you, Nate."

"Don't I know it? And what if you did? Guess I'm big enough to stand it. You just talk to me all you feel like; but see here, little girl, I wouldn't be talkin' to nobody else—I wouldn't."

"Not to Marry?"

"Oh well, that French woman don't so much matter, 'cause most folks wouldn't understand even if she tried to tattle, and I guess she don't. But not to Mis' Hemphill—she's a most su'prisin' gossip, ye know—nor to the Murfrees, nor

Flahertys, nor nobody. These is fam'ly affairs, Lucy, and they ain't for public ears. I'm going down to Lon's now, and your pa'll get home soon—very soon. I'll see to that," grimly. "Now, good night, and don't you shed another tear, will ye?"

He patted her shoulder kindly as he stepped past her, and Lucy looked up with grateful eyes.

"If he's off, Nate, will you come with him?" she whispered fearfully.

"Bet yer life!" was the emphatic answer as he lumbered away on great clumping shoes, true knight as any that used to ride away on a horse just as clumsily arrayed in armor, and perhaps that romantic rider was no better equipped in mind or heart than this glass-blower of the nineteenth century.

CHAPTER VIII

LITTLETON REVIEWED

There never was a truth more tersely expressed than in the vulgar old proverb, "Money makes the mare go." Before Joyce's energy and Joyce's dollars work progressed with rapid strides, and Littleton, as seen on a certain June morning of that year, would never have suggested the bare, ugly collection of buildings she had visited the March before. They had turned the flat sandy plain into a grassy park, with little cottages of picturesque exterior set down all over it at random, apparently, for they faced in all directions; while the green-bordered highways wound in and out among them, like satin ribbon with a velvet edge. Even the Works, themselves, were in the midst of a level lawn, and that part which had been seamed and gullied with footpaths winding about among heaps of sand, or unsightly refuse of fruit and broken glass, was now neatly paved wherever there was no opportunity for verdure to grow.

The two long rows of ugly houses were no more. They had been disintegrated, so to speak; some turned this way, some that, and some removed altogether. On those retained for use additions had been built, verandas added, windows enlarged, and many conveniences planned within doors. Trees and vines had also been planted outside, and the inevitable grass-seed sown broadcast. The men had a joke among themselves that young Early had been obliged to take a seed-store on a debt, and was thus disposing of his stock. The "flat-iron," once watched with a wondering hope, had become a park in truth, the young trees growing healthily in the open space upon which the houses looked, while flower-beds were all abloom. Here and there were benches by the broad walks, and at the narrower end a light wire fence guarded a considerable space, over which was set the sign,

"CHILDREN'S PLAY-GROUND."

Here the turf could not be so well kept, for there were swings, teeters, small man-power merry-go-rounds, and an enticing pond of wading depth, where fleets might be sailed in summer, skates made to glide in winter.

At one side a great archway opened into a long and wide covered way, or viaduct in its original sense, where were more swings and trapeze bars, and here the little ones could play on rainy days. This arched tunnel led from the park to a school-house, so pleasant in appearance that every bright window and graceful stairway seemed to extend an invitation to the passing child.

Within were tinted walls with tempting lengths of black-board, charming colored prints hung up in artistic disarray, with globes in the corners, modeling tables in convenient lights, a piano near the rostrum, and the neatest of chairs and desks.

Rufie and Tilly sat in each of these separately, and declared, "if it wasn't for the studying they'd like to live there right along." Mrs. Hemphill, Rachel's mother, also perambulating through with great curiosity, and three small children clinging to her skirts, pronounced it "fine enough, goodness knows, but wait till you see them teachers!" This rather damped the children's enthusiasm, for by Mrs. Hemphill's manner one would have imagined those teachers little less than monsters.

What caused greatest comment, however, was a stately building just opposite the point of the flat-iron, which brought it very close to the center of the town, and but a stone's-throw from the little church, which was the embodied dream of Gus Peters, turning pain into beauty, and making the scars of his burned arms and hands only a record of glorious days and heavenly nights, because at last he had been enabled to put to practical use the talent that was in him.

As the plaintive song of the teakettle may have been but the wail of imprisoned power, until Watts set it free to work out its glorious destiny, so the boy's surly ways had been his own protest against a destiny that seemed enchaining him to an uncongenial work, for which he brought neither love nor patience. In more congenial labor his soul had broadened, his heart grown warmer, his very looks had improved—But we were talking of the great house near the church. This stately pile, with broad halls from which lofty rooms opened on either side, might be a private dwelling on a large scale, to be sure; yet, instead of chambers above, there was one very large apartment with two or three smaller rooms off, that were being fitted up as a kitchen and dressing-rooms. This building proved a puzzle to these work-people. They could not find any use for it, as they strolled by twos and fours through its unfinished expanse. Nate Tierney suggested that young Early was coming here to live, and that this great upper chamber was to be his ball-room, where he could have his routs and banquets, the kitchen being in handy proximity. Most of the villagers accepted this explanation, as nothing better offered, and commented either in pious disdain, or honest envy.

"He'd have to give big parties, to fill this," remarked Hapgood, slipping clumsily about on the polished floor, "and what's he got that stage at t'other end for?"

"Why, the musicianers, of course," declared Nate. "Jim! but it's fine, ain't it?"

"Umph! How some folks can fling theirselves. It makes you feel 't ain't much use of tryin', don't it?"

"Tryin' for what?" laughed Nate. "Big parties? They're welcome to all the fun they can get out en them, Bill. How'd you and I look slidin' and stumblin' around over that floor of glass, anyhow? No siree! Give me that neat little porch you've got, with Lucy's vine a-growin' 'round it. It'll beat this all hollow!"

"Oh well, that ain't bad, to be sure," allowed Hapgood with some reluctance.

"Bad! I should say not."

"Well, I'll own up, Nate, it is an improvement, and Lucy is as chipper over it as can be. To have a settin'-room, too, besides the kitchen, tickles her most to death. But what gets me is the 'lectric lights and no extry charge."

Hapgood's face, which always reddened easily, was now a dazzling hue. He went on excitedly,

"You jest turn 'em on, so—and there you are, light as day and no charges—same old rent and lights flung in!"

"And heatin' too, Bill. You'll sense the meaning o' that more, next winter. Think of nateral gas for us fellows, and cute little stoves and grates; where you can jest turn it on and off

Fannie E. Newberry

with a thumbscrew. No wood splittin' and sawin', no luggin' baskets of coal, no dust, no smoke, no charges. My! Bill, it's 'most too good to b'lieve."

"Look out we don't crow too soon, Nate. It's less'n a month sense we've had it that way, and you don't know; they may tuck it onto us—"

"Dalton says not."

"Perhaps he don't know. Did you ask him?"

"Yes, and he said the new boss was a—a philandroper, or something. He seemed kind of tickled over it, too, as if he thought it was a kind of tomfoolery, or joke, that mightn't last."

"If it's a freak, no more it will."

"Oh well, we'll get the good of it while it does. You can't live any more'n a day to a time, so what's the use worryin'? Summer's here, and the place is gettin' purtier every day, and it just does a feller's heart good to watch them youngsters racin' and shoutin' in that old flat-iron—'member how we felt it never could be a park, and for us? But you see 'tis, and a special place for the young'uns, too. That ought to clinch the thing, I'm sure!"

So they wondered, questioned, and commented, but never thought of connecting these sunny marvels with the hand-some girl, who was occasionally seen strolling about, either with the older woman, who had been ticketed as her old-maid aunt, or with Mr. Dalton, supposed by all to be some distant relative. Joyce had been very careful to act through agents, and though the workmen sometimes thought she showed a "heap of curiosity," they never imagined that it was her little head which planned and originated every detail of the work they carried on. Not that Joyce could really make a plan—that was beyond her. But she and Madame Bonnivel, together, instructed the intelligent architects employed, even down to the minute contrivances for saving work and time, that were introduced into the cottages.

Even Gus Peters had never fathomed the mystery of his own surprising good fortune. Before night had fallen, on the day he was burned, an elderly woman of serene visage had appeared in his bachelor den, and declaring herself a nurse sent by friends, had proceeded to make him more comfortable than he had believed possible, with those aching members touching up every nerve to torture.

She had served him with delicate food and drink, dressed his burns with softest touch, given him some soothing potion, and prepared a daintily clean bed for him to rest in. When he awoke, after the first refreshing sleep in many hours, she was still there, and the room seemed like another place, so restfully clean and orderly had she made it. Gus looked around with contented eyes, which finally fell upon her and lingered there. For the minute he half suspected it was still a dream, and feared to really waken. But, catching his gaze, she smiled and said in an unmistakably wide-awake voice,

"You had a good sleep, didn't you? The worst is over now, and you'll soon mend. It won't be long now to the itching stage."

She laughed pleasantly and went on with her work in a placid way. Gus discovered, with a little shock of surprised delight, that she was darning a sock—could it be his sock? He asked the question with an eagerness that amused her.

"Of course. Why. Are you afraid I'll spoil it?"

Fannie E. Newberry

The humor of this made him laugh also, for the idea of spoiling socks that were little but holes would make any one smile who felt warm, rested, and free from pain.

"How did you happen to come?" he asked again, a bit timidly.

"I was sent," she returned. "It's my business—to nurse those who are not rich. It makes a different profession of it, where one must often be house-keeper and cook, as well as attendant on the sick, you see."

"Yes, indeed. You're good at keeping house, I reckon. It must have looked a mountain to you to get order out of the mess here."

"I've seen worse places. Now, it's about five o'clock and I'll give you some breakfast, and dress your arms. Then, if you feel comfortable, I'll take a nap myself."

"To be sure. And are you going to stay all day?" wistfully.

"Of course, and to-morrow too, perhaps."

She folded her work in deft fashion, putting thimble and thread away in a bag which, in time, became something of a marvel to Gus, who declared a man never wanted anything but she'd find it in that bag; then went about preparing breakfast, and soon Gus was sipping what seemed like nectar to the poor fellow, who was used to decoctions that might have a name, but neither looked nor tasted like any known drink.

"Well, that *is* coffee!" he cried gratefully. "Say, Mrs.—"

"Keep," she interposed quietly.

"Mrs. Keep, I don't like to be prying, but—but, you under-stand, I'm poor? I can't pay much, and you're way up in your business, I see. Perhaps—"

She smiled in motherly fashion.

"Don't bother your head about that. I am paid, and well paid. You are simply to take things as they come, and hurry to get well. I'm glad to see you can eat."

"Eat? It would be a queer man that couldn't with such a breakfast before him! I guess some fairy must have blessed my cradle when I was born. I never knew, before, I was heir to good luck. Well, there might be worse things than burned hands. Now do me up in fresh rags, Mother Keep, and you shall have as long a nap as you like. I won't even sneeze if you say not."

Mother Keep stayed a week, and left Gus well on the way to a perfect cure, with no scars remaining as a record of his awkwardness. She often talked with the lad, finding it easy to probe him. He talked ardently of his one love, the study of architecture, showing her many plans, and explaining how he saved every penny to spend it in lessons at the Institute, and in materials for this absorbing work. One of these plans— that of a small church, simple in design, yet with real elegance of outline and convenience of arrangement, impressed her greatly.

"I wish you would let me take this away with me," she said. "I will return it after a little."

Gus, who would have almost taken off one of the fast-healing arms for her, had she asked it, assented at once, inwardly hoping she would not soil the beautiful drawing, nor, womanlike, forget all about returning it. When she left,

Fannie E. Newberry

it went with her, and Gus missed both the woman and the drawing that evening. He might indeed have been really melancholy, but some of the boys came in and rather drove away the gentler thoughts of the past few days in their noisy mirth and games.

Still, something of that gentle influence lingered. Gus tempted Rufie with a penny, and coaxed her into brushing up the floor now and then, while he took to hanging up his discarded garments, rather than dropping them in a heap. It was a few evenings later, and he had begun using the least burned hand to some purpose, when a strange man called, and asked if he ever submitted plans in competition. Peters rather mournfully confessed that he had, but with little success, except in one instance, when he had taken a prize in an amateur competition. After a talk on such matters the stranger mentioned, as if incidentally, that plans were requested for a small church about to be built in Littleton; why did not Peters compete? Instantly the young man's thought flew to his drawings, now in Mother Keep's possession. If he had those he might venture. But could he not reproduce them? Oh! if his hands were only well. If Mother Keep would but remember what was of so little consequence to her, but so much to him.

He lay awake long, that night, dreaming dreams of future success, but awoke to a disheartening sense of pain and impotence. There were no letter-carriers in the village, and Gus seldom had reason for frequenting the post-office unless on a bright day, to meet the girls. As he should not begin work to-day, however, he thought he would stroll in that direction. The office, a mere box in one corner of a provision store, was presided over by a woman in spectacles, the wife of the store-keeper. As Gus stood leaning against the side of the door, one arm still in bandages and a sling, a figure entered, passing him quickly by, as if intent on business. He recognized Miss Lavillotte, who had been so kind to him the day he was burned, and waited patiently till she should turn from the little office window, and give him greeting.

Presently she did turn; then, after a quick, intent look, advanced smilingly.

"You are much better?" She asked eagerly. "You look almost well."

"I am, thank you! I had fine care, you see."

"Did you? That was good!"

"I should say! The queer thing is, I don't know where she came from, nor where she's gone to."

"Who?"

"Mother Keep—as I call her. She was fine! She'd cure anything, I reckon."

Joyce laughed, her eyes shining.

"And she really saved you some suffering?"

"She made me almost enjoy it!" laughing blithely. "I wish she'd write to me. I'd like to know her address."

"Perhaps she has. Have you inquired?"

"Goodness! no. I never thought to. Do you suppose she would?"

"I'm not supposed to know much about her, but if, as you say, she was kind I should think she'd feel enough interested to write and ask how you are getting along without her. Shouldn't you?"

"Possibly. I'm going to inquire, anyhow. Say, Mrs. Blake, got anything for Augustus F. Peters this morning?"

The woman slid a small package of letters through her fingers, as she answered,

"Yes, two things if I ain't mistaken. Here's the letter, and I'll find the roll in a minute."

"Aha! Good! I was afraid she'd forget that. It must be my drawings."

"Your drawings?" asked Joyce interestedly. "Are you an artist, then?"

"No. But I'd like to be an architect. They are some plans of a little church that I've been working on a long time. I never expected to make anything out of them, only practice, but—"

He hesitated and Joyce looked up, inquiring and sympathetic. He gave a little choke and continued:

"Well, they say young Early means to build a church here and has called for plans and specifications. Guess it's advertised in some of the papers, but I don't take any. So I thought I'd submit mine—though it won't be any use, I presume. Still, it's worth trying."

"It's always worth trying. I certainly should. And, do you know, I'm a bit interested in the study of architecture myself, and have some books. Wouldn't you like to look them over, now you're unable to work? You're welcome to them for as long as you like to study them."

"Wouldn't I like them! If you knew how I've wanted to get hold of such things, but they cost awfully. I'll be careful, Miss Lavillotte, and put strong paper covers on them. You're sure you'd just as soon let me have them?"

He was like a boy in his enthusiastic joy.

"Perfectly sure. Will you come around, or shall I send them? Come to think, I'll do the latter when Gilbert has the carriage out, this afternoon. They are large and heavy. And don't fail to send in your plans; I shall be anxious to hear if you succeed."

She tripped out, while Gus watched her, an odd expression on his face. Then turning to the woman who was holding out the precious roll, he said bluntly,

"It don't cost a thing to give a man a kind and hopeful word, but how many girls like that would do it? She's a lady!"

He walked away as if on air. He was no longer the awkward lout, stolidly working at uncongenial toil. He had a hope, a purpose, a plan, and his sometimes sullen face was transformed into manly alertness and strength.

From that time on he forgot his burns, and Nature took them in hand, healing the broken flesh in her most clean cut fashion. Scarcely a scar remained, and on the day he received the brief notice that his plans were accepted it seemed as if the scars fell from his soul also, leaving it cleaner, stronger, better. He had found his rightful work, and that is inspiration to any man.

CHAPTER IX

DAN

Factory hours were over, and Dan Price issued from the heated place, his old coat over his arm, and his neck bared to what little breeze there was, as he turned his moist face in the direction of home. There was no loitering among the boys, no waiting for any special girl.

Dan had no boon companions, no home ties, no courting to carry on. He "kept company" with no one but himself. The one room he called home was in one of the houses still untouched by the changes going on, a remnant of the once ugly row, now largely broken into, but not wholly destroyed.

For, with that perversity of inanimate things which attends every large enterprise to retard in every possible manner, through bad weather, the non-arrival of needed materials, loss, breakage, accident, and the "soldiering" of the workmen, many hindrances had arisen, and while wonders had been accomplished much remained to be done. But what had tried Joyce almost beyond endurance was to find that her greatest opposition came from the people she was trying to benefit. Often she found herself, through her builders, butting against a wall of human perversity and stupidity fairly insurmountable.

More than one family, and these in the poorest homes, utterly refused to allow of any improvements, resisting the entrance of the workmen, as if this were an armed incursion of some enemy. In vain Dalton explained that it was only to make them more comfortable, that it should not cost them a penny, that the discomforts of a week, a month, would change their barracks into modern homes. They sullenly defied him to interfere, and would none of these "new-fangled notions" he tried to describe in glowing terms.

"'Tain't fair, boss, and we ain't going to stand it!" shouted one man from his door-step, rotting from the misdirected leakage of the roof. "If we keep the rent paid up you've no right to disturb us in our own homes. If we want changes, or improvements, we'll let you know quick enough. Till we do just let us alone, can't ye? It's all we ask."

Even Dalton, between the Scylla of Joyce's determination and the Charybdis of her people's perversity, sometimes lost his temper entirely, and could do nothing but anathematize them for a "pesky set of fools" right to their faces. So a part of the old buildings still remained, and in Bachelor's Row, where the rooms were mostly let to men without families, lived Dan, forlornest of all in the block. It seemed, to-day, as if the bare, paintless shanties looked worse than ever, by contrast with their improved surroundings, while an air of neglect and disheartenment lingered about them, impalpable but as plainly perceived as an odor. Naked, shutterless, porchless, and hot, they stood in the blazing afternoon sunshine, as obtrusive as the wart on a man's nose, and as ugly. When Dan's dark gaze was uplifted to them he scowled fiercely, and muttered,

"Out of the frying-pan into the fire! I can never stand it inside, to-night. Guess I'll take to the woods."

He stepped from the small front platform directly into a room which smelled strongly of leather and tobacco, where two oldish men with grizzled beards were sitting—one in an apron, cobbling shoes on the bench by the one window; the other, evidently a caller, close by the open door, reading something from a newspaper and gesticulating rather wildly. A sardonic gleam flashed across Dan's handsome face as he passed them with a nod, and disappeared in the room beyond. This was his own, where he stinted himself in other ways that he might keep it unshared, thus insuring the strict privacy he courted.

It was very small and its boards were bare, but he had saved space by making himself a bunk, in lieu of a bed, which, hung on hinges, could be hooked up out of the way when not in use. For the rest, a couple of chairs, a chest of drawers, and a table with a little oil stove for cooking purposes composed the meagre furnishings. But each bit of wall space was occupied in a manner that astonished one at first glance, for up to the height of four feet were shelves partly filled with books and magazines, while above them, reaching to the ceiling, were fastened pine cases protected by glass, in which were collections of butterflies and beetles arranged in a manner that awoke admiration even in those who knew nothing of entomology. But to-day the room was stifling, and even the stiff beetles on their pins seemed to droop in the fierce glare of the sunshine streaming in.

With an impatient "Whew-w!" Dan went hastily about, selecting such things as he needed for his impromptu camp of a night, and soon was ready; a blanket tightly rolled around net and tackle, and some food in his dinner-pail.

Coming out into the yard through the rear door, he stepped under a rough lean-to of a shed, and soon emerged with his wheel, which, being geared to suit his peculiar form, made him look almost like a caricature when mounted. He fastened his paraphernalia in place, steered it around in front and was just mounting when the man with the newspaper issued from the cobbler's room, talking loudly,

"I tell you, it's no good! Toil and moil every day from your first breath to your last, and what good does it bring you? Independence? Humph! You are as much a slave as any nigger bought for cash. Comfort? A heap of that! You'd be better housed and fed in any county-house. Respect? Get yourself charged with a crime and see whether it's any good to have been an honest, hard-working man. I tell you—"

He stopped and Dan, who had buckled his last strap, looked up to see why. He divined instantly, and that same sardonic smile passed over his face once more. Mr. Dalton was approaching, and the speaker, but now climbing the heights of oratory with the paper flourished like a standard before him, shrank suddenly into himself and seemed to fall away, as if he would annihilate himself if he could. Finding that impossible he sank into his chair and began a vague remark about the shoe his host was half-soling, all which the latter took as a matter-of-course, not seeming to notice, even.

Dan pedaled away, laughing harshly.

"Fool!" he muttered. "One would think, to hear him, he was the only one not a coward amongst us, when the truth is he's the biggest one of all. Old Tonguey Murfree would cringe to the devil for ten cents worth of patronage, and then cheat him out of half of it, if he could."

He made his wheel fly in a sort of frenzy of disgust, but the fresh wind, sweeping his hot face like the besom of peace, soon drove away this temporary chagrin, bringing to him the best comfort life gave in those days—the gentle influence of

Fannie E. Newberry

Nature. For, just in proportion as Dan shunned humanity he courted her, and though he felt her relentlessness through every fibre of his suffering being, he felt her charm as well, and could not quite resist it.

He rode fast and far, till the level road, through a turn or two, brought him into a well-wooded tract where bluffs and willow clumps suggested running streams. He left the road and, dismounting, guided his wheel between projecting roots and stumps, down through a winding cow-path which led to a lick below. Here, discarding shoes and stockings he waded the stream, and entered a charming dell where nature had been lavish of adornment. In fact, one might almost have thought time and human ingenuity had assisted nature, for a wild grapevine was so linked from bough to bough between two tall trees as to form a perfect bower, and as if to protect the opening from intrusive onlookers, a sort of *chevaux-de-frise* of tall ferns waved their graceful banners up to meet the drooping lengths of vine waving from the tree.

Toward this bower Dan bent accustomed steps, sliding his wheel into a copse of young oaks that hid it completely, then parting the growing ferns, as if he needed no guide to tell him just where the well-concealed opening might be. As he, stooping, entered, the graceful fronds sprang back to position, like sentinels who have separated an instant to let the master pass, but quickly resume place to guard his hidden presence well.

Inside, Dan glanced about and saw with pleased eyes the undisturbed, familiar aspect of the spot. In one corner was a large heap of dry leaves, which might have drifted there last Fall, but did not, and in any case made an excellent bed for a camper. In another, an innocent-looking tree-root projected from the earth. With a quick jerk Dan dislodged it, showing an excavation below, which had been neatly walled in with stones. Removing the largest one, at the bottom, he disclosed a rough box sunken in the soil, from the compartments of which he drew forth all the articles he needed for his simple supper—an old coffee-pot, an alcohol lamp with its attendant rubber-corked bottle, a frying-pan of small dimensions, a can of shaved bacon, salt, pepper, and so on.

By this time a look of peace, yes, even a sort of tame joy, had replaced Dan's gloomy expression, and one could see that, in a way, he was happy. Getting out his fishing-rod from its enveloping blanket he presently emerged, recrossed the stream, and soon could be seen pushing out into the midst of it, poling an old punt up stream. Anchoring presently in a small cove where the water was deep and cool, he sat in silent watchfulness, occasionally jerking out a perch bass, sometimes a pickerel, but for the most part so still he might have been the occupant of a "painted boat upon a painted" stream. Yet all the time the soft influences of the hour and place were weaving their spell about him. The sun was now only a great half-round of red upon the horizon's line, and way up to the zenith tiny clouds that were like sheep in a meadow caught here and there its scarlet tinge. It was very still, yet all alive with woodsy sounds. Now a belated cicada swung his rattle as if in a fright, next a bull-frog, with hoarse kerchug! took a header for his evening bath. Once, later on, when the shadows were falling, a sleepy thrush settled upon a twig near by, and sang his good-night in sweetest tones. About this time he heard a farm-boy calling anxiously through the neighboring wood for the lost Sukey of the herd, and at times a dusty rumble announced a wagon jolting homeward over the unseen road away to his right. Dan's sense of satisfaction was possibly heightened by this mingling of nearness and remoteness. He had all life at his ear, so to speak, yet held it back by his will, as one might listen at the receiver of a telephone and yet refuse to yield up one's own presence by opening the lips in response. And here

Fannie E. Newberry

there was no "central" to cut him off, though he held the situation long.

At last, in the soft dusk, which wrapped him like a mother's arms, he poled noiselessly down stream, secured the punt, dressed his fish with the dexterity of a practised woodsman, and washing them neatly in the river, waded back to his camp. Again the root handle was lifted, the alcohol lamp filled and lighted, and while the coffee boiled over that, the fish, laid on the slices of bacon, were set to sizzle comfortably over a tiny fire of sticks and leaves built in the stony hollow. Dan was hungry and ate with keen relish. He had produced knife, fork and spoon from his sunken cupboard, but his frying-pan served for both plate and platter, and the cover of his dinner-pail for cup. The bread and doughnuts he had brought from home helped out the repast, which had all the relish and wholesomeness of the out-door meal which has been foraged for by personal effort.

Oddly enough in these tobacco-ridden days, Dan did not smoke. When he had neatly cleaned away the remnants of his feast and replaced root and stone, he spread his blanket out under the stars, and tucking one rolled-up corner under his head for a pillow, lay long into the night, gazing up into the heavens which formed his only roof.

It was a moonlighted evening, and the fleecy clouds we have noted moved in and out of her path in a stately dance, with winning grace, as eastern Nautch girls might dance their way into the favor of a haughty sheik.

Dan at first saw all, but reflected nothing of this beauty in his thought. His animal nature satisfied, he craved nothing as yet. But presently memory and remorse knocked for admittance—the twain were seldom long banished. They sat like skeletons at every banquet. At a bound thought flew back to that day when his brother had fallen before his eyes.

Dan groaned as the awful vision loomed before him. He saw again the trickling blood, the strange, astonished protest on that dying face, with its eyes turned up to his. That was what he could not bear—that Will should have believed he did it, even in carelessness. If the unspoken reproach of that last minute could be removed Dan felt he would be a free man once more. But that hung over him like a curse.

"I didn't do it, Will!" he moaned half aloud. "I wasn't even fooling with the trigger, as you thought. If I'd been careless in that way—but I wasn't. I never see a gun without thinking it may be loaded, and though we both believed that one wasn't still I was careful. But it caught either in your sleeve or mine—nobody will ever know, and it killed you and left me to live on. Who did it, Will? It wasn't you; it wasn't me. Was it the devil, or was it God himself? What is that awful Something that makes things happen just when you're guarding against 'em? For that's what I was doing. I had just looked up to caution you when you pressed so close, and then came the stroke!" He groaned again, as if in physical pain, then presently went on in a moaning voice: "Oh, Will, if you can hear me, believe me and not what other folks may say. They all believe it was me, but that I was so crazy over it I couldn't bear to own up; and the doctor bid them let me alone or I should go mad. But Will, it is not true. You must hear me, wherever you are. *It is not true!*"

He broke into a passion of sobs, and rolling over, muffled his face in the blanket's folds. Even in that solitude some living being might hear, and the thought that anyone should ever witness this agony of soul, should ever lay the lightest touch upon that sacred wound, was torture to him.

Poverty, orphanage, and physical weakness had always set

Fannie E. Newberry

him apart, but while Will lived he had not greatly minded. He had kept in touch with his world through its greatest favorite, that handsome, witty brother; and it had been the same when Will was praised, or courted, as if it had been himself. Death had torn from him the best part of himself, and as if this loss were not cruel enough simply as a loss, it had left behind the conviction that in dying that worshiped brother believed the one who would gladly have died for him to be his slayer. No wonder Dan moaned and writhed, incapable of comfort. He wonder he shunned everybody, knowing what they believed of him.

No wonder he groped in black despair and could not yet look up, or listen to the voices of consolation that might have come to him in different moods.

It was night for Dan in more senses than one.

CHAPTER X

AT THE BONNIVELS'

The Bonnivels were at dinner, one evening, somewhat before the events related in the past few pages, and were discussing in lively tones a long letter which had come from Leon that day—Leon Bonnivel, the absent son and brother who was in a ship of war off the South Atlantic coast. He had just been advanced to a first lieutenancy, and the family were jubilant in consequence.

For the Bonnivels had known hard times in their southern home, when Dorette and Leon were little, and his appointment to the Naval school had been the first lightening of their fortunes, Dorette's marriage to an honest young fellow in a good situation the second.

That Madame Bonnivel and Camille were never allowed to feel their dependence upon Mr. and Mrs. Larrimer Driscoll took from its bitterness, yet it was to Leon both looked as the family's true head, by whose advancement all would certainly be gainers. They loved the spirited young soldier-sailor as helpless women do love their braves, who go out from them to fight the battles of life, and they watched his career with their hearts' pendulums swinging between pride and dread—joy and alarm.

Madame Bonnivel's face was now radiant, while her sightless eyes sparkle with enthusiasm. Dorette looked placidly pleased, Larry kindly sympathetic, while Camille showed her delight in her rattling tongue and eager gestures. "We must tell Joyce," she cried, squeezing Dodo's arm in a vain effort to express all she felt. "She is as fond of him as we are. Maman, how old was she when the Earlys came to board with us?"

"About two, and the dearest baby!" answered Madame with readiness, for next to talking of Leon she loved to talk of Joyce. "Her poor mother even then was marked for death, and when she passed away, during one of her husband's frequent absences, I took her baby right into my arms and heart."

"And Leon must have been about five then?"

"Half-past five, as he used to say, and Dorette here was seven. Such a houseful of babies!"

"Luckily I had not appeared on the scene then," laughed Camille. "I'm afraid I was not a welcome guest."

Her mother turned fond, reproving eyes upon her, while Dodo broke in between big mouthfuls of oatmeal and milk,

"But me was dere, jus' de same. Me 'members all about it."

"Oh, you remember more than the rest of us have forgotten!" cried her auntie, catching the child's chubby arm and shaking little trills of merriment out of her, at which the young father exclaimed with mock savagery.

"Will you never leave that child alone, Gypsy? You're always squeezing or pinching her."

"But I lubs her so!" with a shower of pats and punchings. "I could eat her up."

"Better stick to your dinner—it's a good one! My wife is chef of this establishment."

Dorette's soft eyes met his in a fond, merry glance.

"Thank you, Larry! You always appreciate good things."

"Don't I, though! But go on, mother. You were telling us about the babies."

"You know it all as well as I. We loved little Joyce as our very own, and when her father took her away—for somehow he never liked us, I think because I once spoke too plainly about his neglect of his delicate wife—when he took her to a woman he had engaged to look after her, she moaned and cried in the most pitiful way, refusing all food and begging day and night for 'ma mere,' as she had learned to call me. Nothing would pacify her, and at length in desperation he brought her back. We were poor then, but I did not receive her because of the board money he would pay—"

"Did you keep it in a ginger-jar, Mother?" put in Larry, with a chuckle. She caught his meaning quickly, and returned at once,

"I was about to add, because I knew from past experience there would be little of it to hoard, even in a ginger-jar. James Early was not as prompt a payer as collector," dryly. "No, I took back my baby because we all missed her so, especially Leon, who had wailed all day and half the night, calling on 'Doyce! Doyce!' even in his dreams, poor little man! It was the end of the second day when Mr. Early, looking decidedly sheepish, reappeared with his little daughter—about this time, in fact. I can see, even now, the look of perfect rest and happiness upon her tear-stained little face as she nestled into my arms that evening, while Leon and you, Dorette, fairly radiant with joy, bent above her. I never saw one of you show one moment's jealousy, which was a bit odd, for Joyce was an imperious baby, and exacted a great deal of my attention. But how charming was her good-nature! That night she sat throned on my knees, like a little princess, and patty-caked, threw kisses, went to mill and to meeting, and said over her whole short vocabulary of French and English words, so gracious and lovely that even your studious father pushed back his books and papers to join the frolic. We were wonderfully happy that night! I think the child is magnetic. She gives out her own happiness like electric sparks. She never can bottle it up and enjoy it selfishly."

"And she stayed till she was fifteen?"

"Yes. Then her father began to make money, and he made it—"

"Hand-over-fist," interposed Larry.

"Exactly. And I never saw one so puffed up with pride and vain-glory. It would have been funny, only that he made us feel it so tragically. He tore Joyce away—the word is not an exaggeration for she fought him at every point and only yielded to positive compulsion. He put her into a fashionable school and bade her have nothing more to do with those 'down-at-the-heel Bonnivels.' It was a trifle hard after the love and care we had lavished upon her."

"It was beastly!" muttered Larry between his shut teeth. "Did he never give you even gratitude, let alone money?"

"No. He measured out a niggardly sum for her board, and

gave it over with the air of munificently rewarding me. I would have refused to accept it, but your father was gone, then, and I nearly blind. I could not let my little ones suffer to gratify my own pride. I took it, but I dared not speak for fear I should say too much. I simply bowed my head in acknowledgment, and thanked God when he was gone, because I had been able to control myself!"

"But Joyce did not see that?" put in Dorette.

"No, I am glad to say she did not. The scene with her had ended with her passionate rush to the carriage, where she was lying back on the seat half fainting amid her tears."

"Oh, how cruel!" cried Camille, almost in tears herself.

"And when you had gone blind through your constant embroidering to keep your little tribe together—Joyce and all!"

"Never mind, dear! Larry came then and saved us all."

She turned a sweet glance upon her son-in-law, which made him flush with pleasure.

"I don't know about that saving process, mother. I've pretty often declared in my own mind that Dorette and you came along just in the nick of time to save *me*."

"Me too," put in Dodo, insistent on general principles.

"And me!" added Camille, laughing and squeezing the baby afresh, her moods as quick to change as those of capricious April, always.

"Yes, the whole shirackety of you," returned Larry, folding

his napkin. "And Joyce has made amends since, I'm sure."

"Indeed she has, dear child!"

"But mother, even Joyce has never given—"

"Hush, Camille! Don't say it. Joyce knows we are entirely comfortable, and she has large plans to carry out. She gives us unstinted love and gratitude. Joyce has never failed me yet."

Camille was silenced. She caught Dodo out of her high chair, and made the movement from table general.

They had scarcely reached the homelike living-room when the doorbell sounded a quick peal that rang through the house. It made the Madame exclaim,

"Why, that sounds like her now!" and, sure enough, in a moment Joyce stood, laughing, in their midst.

"Are you glad to see me?" she cried merrily, passing her greetings about, but returning to the mother's side directly. "I had Gilbert bring me over, for I've something to talk about; and may I stay all night?"

A universal cry of assent having answered her, she turned, with her brightest smile, to Larry.

"Will the honorable householder dismiss my coachman, then?" and as, with an exaggerated bow and flourish, he disappeared to execute the commission, she turned swiftly upon Madame Bonnivel. "Ma mere, aren't you paler than you should be? What is the matter?"

"I've had just a trifle of a headache, cherie, nothing worth mentioning."

"I don't like those headaches—do see Dodo! Her eyes are falling asleep while she is running about; if she stops one instant she'll be a goner!"

All laughed as the child opened her drooping lids to their widest, and declared she "was dest as wide awake as a hen," but papa, who had re-entered, caught her regardless of protests.

"I'll put her to bed, Dorette. You stay and visit, but don't, Joyce, tell quite all you know till I get back. Come, Sleepyhead! Papa'll tell about the little red hen"—aside to Joyce—"It's my stock yarn. Couldn't tell another to save my head, and studied that out, word for word, on purpose. But luckily she wants it every time. I should be bankrupt if she didn't. Come now, say good-night to all like a lady, Toddlekins."

"Oh, don't bother her, Larry. Joyce can take the ceremony for granted," put in the affectionate aunt, who could not bear that any should tease baby except herself.

"Yes, there's my kiss," throwing it, "and don't get her roused up, Larry. I've things to discuss."

"All right. We go, but I return. *Au revoir.* And talk woman's foolishness till I get back—do! I want to be here when you get off the latest fallals."

But she began tamely enough.

"I saw something in the paper the other day that I want to ask about. Is it your house here that is advertised for sale?"

Madame Bonnivel nodded, and Dorette answered,

"Yes, isn't it too bad? The owner has died and the estate is to be turned into money wherever possible. We can stay until it is sold, or can leave by giving a fortnight's notice at any time, if we prefer."

"And then where will you go?"

"Oh, we haven't planned that far," said Camille. "I say, let it be in the suburbs. I hate to think of an apartment, again."

"But, my dear, there are far pleasanter ones than we used to know," put in her mother gently. "I do regret leaving here, though. It will be difficult to find another place, within our means, where we will find so much room out-doors and in. Poor Dodo will miss the grassy yard."

"And Dodo's grandmother, too," added Camille. "You ought to see how chummy they are, Joyce, out under our one maple."

Joyce was looking at that spiritual woman with an expression that arrested the girl's thought and words. It was the look of one who longs, hopes, yet fears, and mingled withal was that adoring fondness she often showed this mother of her heart.

"I see, ma mere. You cannot go into an apartment. It would mean imprisonment for you. And so—and so—oh! I don't know just how to get it out, but—I have had two of the houses at Littleton especially fitted up, and they are close together in what will soon be a great lawn. They are very much alike, but altogether different—that is, they are just different enough not to be tiresomely similar and—where was I?"

All broke into laughter. Joyce's confusion was too funny.

"I think you were in either a maze of syntax, or of building-lots; I scarcely know which," remarked the Madame, evidently overflowing.

"Well, there are two houses—that is sure. One is for me, and the other"—she looked all about with a beautiful smile, nodded brightly at Larry who appeared opportunely in the doorway, and laid a tender hand on Madame's knee—"the other is for ma mere, if she will only be good enough to live close beside her naughty baby, and help her along in life."

"Oh, Joyce! Joyce," cried that lady, catching the hand between her own, while with a sharp little sound Camille sprang to her feet, Dorette meanwhile breaking into a laugh almost like Dodo's for innocent joy.

"I knew you, Joyce!" said she, and Madame, caressing the girl's hand, added tremulously, "My dear, dear child!"

"And so I'm no longer to be proprietor and boss," cried Larry, coming forward. "Oh, I've heard you plotting and planning. Mother Bonnivel, are you going to turn us Driscolls out of doors, now you've come into your palace?"

"Oh dear, no palace! Just a comfortable home with room enough to swing all Dodo's kittens in," laughed Joyce, to keep back the tears, for the dear mother's joy upset her.

"I should dread a palace, cherie," said the latter, then turned to the young husband of her daughter, whom she loved as a son. "We've had no mine and thine so far, Larrimer, and we won't begin now."

"Oh!" was Camille's outburst, "how perfectly charming it is to have it come from Joyce. If it was anybody else mother could never be induced to take it. Do tell us more, Joycey

Fannie E. Newberry

love—how far out is Littleton by rail? Could Larry live there and go in to his work? Could I go on with my music and cadet teaching?"

"It is forty minutes ride by rail. You saw the town before anything was done and in early spring. You would not know it now. It is green where it was brown, clean where it was dirty, trim where it was shabby. It begins to look like a great park, and the cottages are really ornamental, as well as comfortable. Our homes are to overlook the town and face the park at its broad end—you know it is triangular in shape—and they are already at the decorating stage. I did not want to go further without letting the rest of you have your say."

"Oh, delicious!" cried Camille. "I do think planning out pretty rooms is perfectly fascinating. Can't you tell us something how they are built?"

Joyce laughed, and took from her pocket a large sheet of letter paper, looking meanwhile with half suffused eyes towards Madame.

"Do you remember, ma mere," she said tenderly, "how we used to sew and plan together in those old days when we were so poor in money and so rich in dreams?"

"Indeed I do, Joyce."

"And, one winter's day, when the house was so cold we had to huddle close around the old wood stove and shiver, do you remember telling how we would have our home if we could, and how perfectly it should be warmed in winter and cooled in summer? We all got enthusiastic over it; there were you and Dorette and I, while Camille lay fast asleep in her cradle; and first one, then another, would propose some convenience, until we forgot the cold entirely. Finally you cried gaily, 'Wait, I'll draw a plan. These are good ideas for somebody, if not for us. Give me a pencil and paper Joyce,' and presently you showed us what you had drawn."

"Oh, yes! The pretty house with the dumb waiter going from cellar to attic, and the soiled clothes dump from the upper floors to the laundry, and the store-room down-stairs for trunks and heavy furniture, and—"

"And the long drawers under the deep window-seats for best gowns," broke in Dorette with unusual excitement, "and the little cedar closet for furs, and the elegant lighted closets. I remember the plan perfectly. But that—is that it, Joyce?"

"This is the very self-same drawing," said the latter merrily.

"I had wondered what became of it, then forgot it entirely," laughed the Madame. "So you have had it all the time?"

"Yes, I stole it. And, ma mere, the house is built. There are the very little nooks, sunny and warm, that you planned in the library for reading and writing; the pretty Dutch kitchen with its long low window, and the central hall with its wide fireplace. They are all real now, not a dream any more. And they are yours. You have only to take possession, after giving a few orders to the decorators about colors, and so forth. If you say so, Gilbert shall drive us out to-morrow. We can take Dodo, and carry a luncheon to picnic by the wayside. It will be a lovely outing. Won't we, everybody?"

But somehow words came tardily just then. Larry had caught Joyce's hand, and was pumping it up and down somewhat wildly, while his lips quivered under his mustache; Madame Bonnivel had a trembling grasp upon the other hand, while Dorette and Camille were each kissing an ear, or an eye— they could not see for tears and did not care anyhow, so long as it was a bit of Joyce. Till, flinging her arms about them all, she broke out into a sudden passionate, "Oh, dear people! *My* people! Let's cling together. I've nobody in all the world but you!" At which heart-breaking cry the mother quickly responded,

"Why, child, you are a part of us. We have had you always when we could. Do you suppose we would ever let you go?"

So Joyce turned her giving into begging, and in assuring her of the love and loyalty she longed for, all forgot their words of thanks till Larry said whimsically, "I'm afraid things are getting a little mixed here, and I'm not quite certain, now, whether we're to be grateful to Joyce for a beautiful home, or she to us for deigning to live beside her."

This set Camille off into a near approach to hysterics, and let them all gently down to earth once more.

Presently the Madame began in her tender voice, which could never seem to interrupt,

"We haven't told our news yet, Joyce. It pales a little before your grand tidings, but I think it will interest you still. Leon has been promoted."

Joyce turned quickly, her face all aglow, her eyes like stars.

"Oh, is it true? Then he is first lieutenant?"

"Yes, with special work in the engineering department, and such kind words from his higher officers in their congratulations! We had thought our cup of joy quite full when you came in; now it has overflowed."

"And mother was telling all about you and Leon when you

were little," put in Camille in so oblivious a tone that Larry, catching some fun in the situation, laughed outright.

"What a giggler you are, Larry! Just like a school-boy," admonished the gypsy-maid, frowning at him. "What she said about their childish devotion was very touching, I thought, and not at all funny."

Even Madame Bonnivel joined in his hearty laugh, now, and poor Joyce, to hide her burning cheeks, broke out,

"Come, Camille, where's your mandolin? I haven't heard you play for an age. 'Do let's play and be cheerful!'"

"Just what Leon always used to say! All right, I'll give you my last serenade; it's awfully sweet. Turn down the lights, Larry. Now, you must all imagine you are on the water in Venice, and that I'm stealing by in my gondola to call up my lady, love from sleep. She's up in the tower-room of that dingy old castle yonder. Hus-sh all!"

They were silent in the dim room, but Joyce's heart was still beating hard. Would Leon be as pleased as they? She hoped they would tell him in just the right way, he was so proud, and on the dainty "tinkle-tinkle-tum" of the stringed instrument her thoughts floated outward over the broad sea, to find her childhood's mate again.

CHAPTER XI

THE SOCIAL HOUSE

The large building which had caused so much comment was at length finished, and the mystery solved. It was indeed a mansion, with rooms for recreation and study, but it was neither for young Early, nor any other one person. It was, instead, the joint property of all the village, and to be known as the Littleton Social House. On the lower floor was a library, with well-lighted nooks, to be used as reading-rooms; beyond that were the art-rooms one for modeling in clay, one for sketching, and a third inner, sky-lighted, place for photography. On the other side of the great hall was a large music-room with a canvas floor, containing a piano and cabinet organ, also shelves for music numbers, and a raised dais for art orchestra. Beyond was a pleasant parlor, from which opened a small apartment provided with conveniences for quiet table games; and all these were neatly fitted with strong easy chairs, tables, and cabinets, the walls being beautified with many good photographs from paintings of masters, both old and new.

The supposed "ball-room," above, developed into a gymnasium and entertainment hall, with a rostrum and curtains, where lectures, concerts, pictured views, and little dramas might be given; and surrounding this were roof balconies, with palms, vines, and potted plants, making them into bowers of beauty and coolness. Here were seats and tables where the warm and weary might stray for a cooling drink of lemonade, or an ice, served at a price within the means of the very poor. A trim little widow, whose husband when living had been a trusted employee, and who was trying her best to raise her young family without him, had been set up in this restaurant, apparently by Mr. Dalton, and provided with the necessary outfit, for which she was to pay a living rental during the summer months. The chance seemed heaven-sent to the poor young creature, who had nearly succumbed before her heavy toil at the washtub, for she was too delicately formed for such labors.

The janitorship of the whole large building brought independence to another family where the capable mother dying had left a crippled husband and two young girls to struggle on as best they could. With the youthful help of these sturdy girls he could undertake the office of caretaker, and, as pretty living rooms were furnished them in the high, airy basement, the family felt almost as if they had been transported to Paradise after the terrible experiences of the past winter, with a mere shed for shelter, the coal running short at too frequent intervals, and meat only compassed as a rare luxury on the "lucky" days when one or the other could pick up an extra nickel, or two, by some special good fortune.

To all the questions and conjectures over this miracle of a house Mr. Dalton opposed an impassive front. "It is none of my doing," he averred brusquely. "I never should have thought of it, and wouldn't have built it if I had, no matter who furnished the money, for I don't believe you'll appreciate it, or take care of it. But all I've got to say is, if any one of you do abuse it, and go to spitting on the floor, or hacking up the woodwork, or pulling things out of shape in any way, you'll be lower than any truck that I care to have around, and you'll have me to deal with when I'm at my ugliest—you understand what that means!"

The men, who had been grouped in the yard after hours, talking it over, and whose hail for information as he passed by had brought out his vigorous remarks, looked at each other and grinned half sheepishly. Then one spoke up sturdily:

"I guess we know good manners when we see 'em, boss! We ain't pigs, nor tramps."

Dalton laughed in his curt fashion.

"You know well enough, but you don't care pretty often. If young Early is decent enough to give you boys a chance at some pleasure, you want to show you appreciate it—that's all. And when you get your invite to the house-warming, you'll be expected to show up as the gentlemen you can be when you try."

Billy May, once a sailor, straightened up and touched his cap.

"Ay, ay, sir!" he bellowed, as if receiving orders in a towering gale, at which all laughed and Dalton, smiling in spite of himself, passed on.

The invitations came in good time, and were in a somewhat comprehensive form, each being addressed to the house-holder in person, with the words, "and whole family" added. No family was forgotten, but as the building could not accommodate the whole village, two evenings were set for the reception and opening, all the names up to N, in alphabetical order, being chosen for Tuesday evening and the rest for Wednesday, while different hours were mentioned that there need be no crowding, though it was discovered later that no matter at which hour one arrived, the most of them staid till the very latest mentioned, loth even then to leave the, to them, novel scene.

A day or two before this pleasant event, which had set the whole town into a delightful turmoil of expectation and comment, a couple of families quietly moved into the two neat, but by no means sumptuous dwellings, lately built on the little knoll over against the broad end of the park, and facing it. You will remember that the school-house was at one side, the church near by, while the Social house fronted the narrow point, with a street between. Thus the two homes overlooked park and buildings, exactly facing the Social house, though at a distance, while the Works at the other extreme of the village were half hidden by intervening buildings, and soon would be quite overshadowed by the many trees lately set out.

These were the homes which Joyce had built for herself and the Bonnivels. Both of them, though fitted with many conveniences and finished with taste, were of moderate cost, there being not one extravagance, and only the modicum of room actually needed for refined living, in either. Many a rich woman has thought nothing of putting more expense into the fitting of one room, even, than Joyce had laid out on her whole house. Indeed that reserved for Madame was much the costlier of the two. Yet, with the pretty outlook across the green triangle before the doors, the high situation, the soft roll of the lawns surrounding them, and the majesty of the one immense maple which stood between the buildings, and had grown for a quarter of a century in lordly majesty, appropriating to itself all the juices of the soil for yards around, until it was the famed landmark of that region, these places were more attractive than many more palatial which fairly daunt the stranger with their cold magnificence.

These smiled in one's face with a hospitable welcome.

Moving was not a difficult operation for Joyce, as she had little heavy furniture to take from the hotel; and it had been a labor of love and jollity to run about with Dorette and Camille, selecting and arranging, first submitting everything to Madame's superior and almost faultless judgment. And here the girl's passion for sharing—she liked the word better than giving—often asserted itself. Obstinately declaring that she should be wretched in a home where everything "smelled of its newness," she had coaxed and cajoled her friends until, almost without their realizing it, there had been such a division of the old Bonnivel effects and the new Lavillotte purchases that both houses presented a pretty equal mingling of the ancient and modern. For instance, Joyce begged the small round table with claw legs from their dining-room, to send in its place one of the handsomest large mahogany rounds she could procure. So Ellen's room was neatly furnished with Madame Bonnivel's square heavy set, stately if not graceful, while the latter's bloomed out with pier-glass and satinwood of the daintiest. The Bonnivels' worn cane chairs somehow found places on Joyce's veranda, while a new half-dozen rockers, of quaint and comfortable shape, took their places through the pretty living rooms next door.

"I feel," said Joyce gaily, "so much more respectable than if my things were all new. These good old plantation souvenirs give to my indefinite outlines a deep rich background that brings me out in stronger colors."

For, with all her wealth and power, Joyce often felt this "indefiniteness," as she called it. She knew people were wont to ask, "Who is she? Where is her family?" and to look with some misgiving on a girl too rich to pass unnoticed, yet too poor to own a family and a past about which she was free to babble. She found that riches set one out from the crowd as does the search-light which cannot be dodged nor dimmed, and sometimes she would have flung every dollar away, and given up all her pet schemes, just to have crept into the safe shelter of the Bonnivel home as a real child of that house, to become as happily obscure as Dorette, or Camille.

The Tuesday night of the first house-warming fortunately fell upon a cool evening, when no one could much mind the occasional sprinkle of rain, so glad were they of a change from the fierce heat and drought of the past fortnight. As it was, the clouds brooded low, and the breeze held the freshness of showers near by, while now and then the moon peered through a rift and lit up the hushed darkness, which was like that of a chamber where sleep comes after pain.

The Social house, gleaming with electric lights to the very summit of the flag-staff above its roof, from which the stars and stripes waved in languid contentment, was not only near the center of the town, geographically, but also in aim and interest, to-night. The half-world which was not invited till to-morrow was anxious to see how the other half would look in gala costume, to-night; and a stranger, suddenly dropped into the neighboring streets, would have had to look twice to convince himself these neat-looking females, tripping that way, were the wives and daughters of artisans who worked for a few shillings a day. Fortunately summer dress-goods cost little, and there were but few of the girls who had not compassed a new six-cent muslin, or at least "done up" an old one into crisp freshness. The men were equally disguised by soap, water, and shaving, with coats instead of shirt-sleeves, but these could not simulate the fine gentleman so readily as could their daughters the fine lady.

Among these self-respecting Americanized families there was occasionally seen a sprinkling of those who disdained any approach to dudishness, or had not yet grasped it as anything that could possibly pertain to themselves, and these—mostly new importations from Poland or Italy— strode dauntlessly up to the wide-open doors in the deep Grecian portico, the men in clumping shoes and the women in little head shawls, jabbering noisily with wonder and curiosity.

Mr. Dalton, under sealed orders, had placed himself, with his aunt, near the outer doorway of the broad entrance hall to receive the guests, and when Joyce's party appeared all were welcomed exactly as had been the other arrivals.

Their entrance was rather imposing, though, despite precautions, for first came Larry with Madame, then Dorette with Joyce, and lastly Camille leading Dodo, with Ellen stalking at their side, the very picture of a duenna. Somewhat in the rear Gilbert and two other maids, Kate and Thyrza— this latter from the Bonnivel house—followed with dubious looks, feeling probably that they were neither "fish flesh, nor good red herring," in this motley assemblage, which offered no such companionship as they were accustomed to.

Joyce's eyes shone like stars, and even in her plain white Suisse gown, without an ornament except the rings upon her fingers, there was a sort of regal splendor about her that made every eye turn to watch her as she entered. After Mrs. Phelps had greeted them all with evident pleasure at having them for neighbors, they found an easy-chair for Madame, where she might listen and feel the happy surging of the crowd about her. As soon as seated she gently pushed Joyce away.

"Go," she whispered. "You want to see and talk with as many as possible. I shall do nicely alone. All of you go, and then you can tell me more when you come back. It will be fun to compare experiences. Who has Dodo?"

"I have her just this minute," said Camille, "but she has sighted Larry and I can't hold her. He is talking to two men in the window at your left, and looking handsome as a picture! There, for goodness' sake, go, if you must! I do believe the little tyke has torn my new dimity, clutching at it so. Come, Joyce, let's go and speak to those girls. They look positively wretched in their best clothes, poor things!"

"You go," said Joyce. "I see my old friend Mrs. Hemphill— Rachel's mother, you know. See her, there with the three children? We must make the most of ourselves, and you can jolly up the girls better than I. I'm going to bring some of the interesting people to you, ma mere. You'll know how to talk to all of them, but you shan't be bored!"

"We need no special vocabulary to be kind," smiled Madame. "I will soon make friends right here, and I'm not afraid of being bored. People always talk to the blind, and smile on the deaf. Run along!"

Joyce gave her a love-pat, and hurried after Mrs. Hemphill who, with a strong grasp on her little ones, was stemming the tide of humanity with a somewhat defiant mien, while her head was swinging around as if on a pivot, so determined was she not to miss the sight of a single decoration or picture, nor the passing of a single guest. She stopped to speak to a much wrinkled dame in a real Irish bonnet, with a flapping frill, who was smiling so broadly as to display with reckless abandon her toothless gums.

"Purty foin, ain't it?" this one laughed, as they stopped abreast of each other so suddenly that the babies nearly fell over backward. "And say," lowering her voice so that Joyce barely caught the words, "they do be tellin' they's to be sand-whiches, an' coffee, an' rale ice-crame byme-by. Does ye b'lave it?"

"Umph! It gets me what to b'lieve, these days," muttered Mrs. Hemphill, with a backward slap at one of the children who, upon hearing the enumeration of goodies, began to tease for some. "What's ailin' you now?" she cried fiercely. "Want somepin to eat, you say? You want a trouncin', that's what you want!" lifting the little thing with a motion tenderer than her words. "Ain't it all the craziest doin's? But say, Mis' Flaherty, they tells me you won't go into one of the new houses, nohow."

"And why should I, tell me thot!" began Mrs. Flaherty on a high key, just as Joyce stepped graciously forward, with the words,

"Isn't this the Mrs. Hemphill I remember?"

The latter turned quickly.

"Hey? Oh, why yes, I do mind you now. Let's see, you come to sell a washin' machine, didn't you? Or was it a story-paper? Oh! no, now I know," darting suspicious glances over the head of the child in her arms, "you was talkin' about schools and tryin' to get one up."

"Well, partly," answered Joyce, rather crestfallen, and glanced up to meet the dancing eyes of Larry, who was passing by and caught the high-keyed sentence. "But you know I have come here to live now, and I assure you I am not a teacher—just a private citizen."

"Do tell! Well, I thought you was something or other—they's sech a raft of agents along; though my Mary tells me 'tain't a circumstance to the city—Mate works out in the city. Let me make you acquainted with Mis' Flaherty. She's the lady what lives in Bachelor's Row and takes in boarders and washin's—now, Johnny, you stop a-tuggin' at my skirts, will ye? You've started the gethers a'ready.—She ain't exactly a bachelor herself, but she's next to it—a widder woman. He! he!"

Mrs. Hemphill's laughter was so much like the "crackling of thorns under a pot" as to be far from pleasant. Joyce hastened to speak.

"But I can't see why you preferred not to move, Mrs. Flaherty. Don't you like the new houses?" she asked, a bit anxiously, looking from one to the other and feeling decidedly wet-blanketed.

"Oh, they'll do," nodding the cap frills vigorously. "It ain't fur the loikes o' me to be sayin' anythin' agin 'em, but I never did take to these new-fangled doin's, 'm. I've heered tell how them water pipes'll be afther busting up with the first frost, just like an old gun, and I don't want any sich doin's on my premises. No *sir*! I ain't so old but I can pump water out of a well yet, and it's handy enough.' 'Tain't more'n just across the strate, and whin 'tain't dusty, nur snowy, nur muddy, it's all right enough."

"Well, I don't carry water when I can make it run by turning a stopple—not much I don't!" cried Mrs. Hemphill vigorously, meanwhile tilting back and forth on heels and toes with a jolting motion which was gradually producing drowsiness in the infant she held. "And my man says it can't freeze in them pipes 'cause the nateral gas is goin' to run day and night and keep 'em hot. And Nate Tierney, he says 't water an' heat an' lightin' is goin' to be jest as free, in our town, as sunshine an' air is everywhere. That's what Nate says, and if it's true it's a mighty big load off 'n us poor folks, and that's certain!"

"But we're goin' to be taxed for 'em," put in another woman, joining the group—a lanky creature with washed-out eyes,

Fannie E. Newberry

and lips that she seemed in danger of swallowing, so sunken were they.

"How's that?" cried Mrs. Hemphill, sharply.

"It's to be some way put onto the men in their drink and tobacco—so my man says—and it'll make it a cent more on a glass and a plug. My man says everybody what brings any into this town's got to pay somethin' fur the privilege, and that goes into the heatin' and lightin' fund. And he says it's a blamed shame, and the men won't stand it, either! Fur's that's concerned, what do they care whether we're warm or cold, so 't they gits their dram?"

Just here Rachel Hemphill came rapidly towards them.

"Mother," she began, then looked askance at Joyce, whose eyes, now somewhat troubled, turned eagerly to meet her glance.

"Well, what is it now?" asked the mother crossly, for, though she liked nothing better than to sit and praise Rachel by the hour, she always kept her belligerent attitude toward her family, as if afraid she might relent too much if she once gave way an inch.

"I was going to say," the girl continued excitedly, with another glance at Joyce, "you'll miss the concert, if you don't hurry. It's upstairs in the big room, and they're all hustling for seats. And mother," dropping to a whisper, "our Kip is to sing!"

"Kip? You don't say! Who told you? Let's hurry! Johnny, come along and stop dragging your feet. I'll lay the babby down some'ers and go right up; he's sound fur an hour or two, I hope. You're coming, Rache?"

"Yes, in a minute," for Joyce had stepped towards her with outstretched hand, partly barring her way.

"My name is Lavillotte," she said, "and I have seen you several times. The Bonnivels and I have just moved into the two houses at the other end of the park, and we want to get acquainted with our neighbors."

Rachel's cool fingers dropped into Joyce's eager jeweled ones, and fell away again.

"You will find but a small set of your kind of people here, Miss Lavillotte. There's the doctor's family, Mr. Dalton's, and one or two others. I'm just one of the working girls," and before Joyce could speak to protest she had turned away with a proud look, and hastened after her mother.

CHAPTER XII

THE HOUSE-WARMING

Joyce had never been used to rebuffs. Feeling like a child who has had its gift of sweeties flung back into its face she turned slowly to retrace her steps towards Madame Bonnivel, and even in the short circuit of the crowded rooms she more than once caught words of criticism and unfriendly comment. One man, who was gesticulating largely with his somewhat grimy hands, uttered these words while she slid and sidled through the unyielding group about him, almost like one trying to avoid a blow—

"Generous! Who says he's generous? Don't you fool yourselves. We'll have to pay for it somehow, you mark my words. Young Early's like his father, only 'cuter. He's going to work things up till he makes folks think this town's a little Eden and then, when more workers wants to come here because it's sort o' neat and pretty, he'll begin to squeeze us on the wages, and if we dare to kick he'll say coolly, 'Go, if you don't like it. There's plenty ready and waiting to take your place.' Oh, I know 'em, root and branch, and we ain't no more'n just a pack o' cards in their hands. They shuffle us, and deal us round where we can help 'em to rake in the most chips, and when they're done with us—pouf! away we go into the fire, for all they care."

Joyce, fairly stung, made a quick movement towards him, then, remembering herself drew back, while the man, turning at the minute, smiled and made way for her. She was only a pretty girl to him, and he had not Rachel's discerning eyes, to observe that she was out of her class here, and never for an instant imagined what his tirade had meant to her.

When Joyce reached the Madame she was trembling a little, and pressed herself against that lady's chair, longing for comfort. Yet, in reply to the Madame's greeting she answered with but one word. She was afraid to trust herself with more. The blind woman's keen instinct divined that something was amiss. She had been talking placidly with many, and had also heard all sorts of comments and conjectures, so could imagine the feelings of this warm-hearted girl who had been giving so freely, and who longed for some little expression of appreciation and gratitude in return. But fearing themselves surrounded she could not speak quite freely, so she clasped Joyce's trembling fingers warmly while she quoted with an arch, smiling face.

"Perhaps it was well to dissemble your love,
But why did you kick me down-stairs?"

Joyce had to laugh heartily amid her gloom, and felt better for the outburst.

"It's what I want to know, myself!" she cried warmly. "Have I quite deserved it all?"

"It's the way of the world, my dear. But I've something to tell you, on my side. I have just been talking to a young girl—I think they call her Lucy—and she is so glad and happy over this house and its possibilities! I wish you could have heard her talk. She says her mother is dead, and she is busy all day with the housework and babies. But to-night some good

Fannie E. Newberry

friend she called Nate, as I remember, who is not invited till to-morrow evening, said he would sit with the children and she should come with her father. It's the first party she was ever at, and she has a new muslin for it, and some dear Marry, as she called her, gave her a bit of nice lace for the neck, and it has been all bliss and rapture! Her voice was fairly tremulous with happiness, Joyce."

"O!" cried the latter, feeling better and better, "It must have been Lucy Hapgood. I wish I could have seen her, myself. Which way did she go?"

"I don't know, dear. Who is near us now? No one very close, is there?"

"No—at least all are busy with their own affairs."

"Then I will say this; remember always that you are not doing these things for gratitude, nor praise. That has always been understood, hasn't it?"

"Yes, yes, of course. But—but it's hard to have abuse, ma mere!"

"They don't mean it for you, cherie. Are they not all nice to you, personally?"

"They treat me well enough, yes. But not as if they really care for me."

"And why should they, on so short acquaintance! Remember, they do not dream who their good fairy really is. And you must always tell yourself it is not *you* they repulse. You simply stand for the class that has oppressed and cheated them. They denounce "young Early" to-night, simply for the sake of what has gone before. They cannot believe in real friendliness all at once, and they look coolly on you, imagining you have no interests in common with them. They look across a gulf of suffering and privation at you, who seem never to suffer, and their eyes grow hard and stony. Can you wonder? You should not be either surprised, or hurt."

"But they don't treat you so, mother. And you are of my class, as you call it."

"Am I? Well, granting all that, you forget I am blind. My affliction brings me more in touch with them. I would have no feeling of superiority—I could not; so they come nearer to me, perhaps. Or else I have fallen among pleasanter people. Look your sweetest now, and try once more. I'm sure you will find some warmer currents in this frozen stream, if you sound it well."

Joyce smilingly pressed the gentle hand that caressed her own.

"I'll make another plunge," she said more hopefully. "Ah! here's Mr. Dalton. I think he looks a bit *triste*, too. Good evening again, Mr. Dalton. I want to ask you a question, please. Can you tell me who is that man with the brown hair and bristling red beard, over in that group by the door— there, he is just moving on."

"That? Oh yes, I see. Why, his name is Hapgood—Bill Hapgood, as we all call him. His girl Lucy is here some-where—a good child, sadly overworked. He's no good, though; always quarreling with his bread and butter, and much too fond of the saloon."

"Lucy Hapgood's father!" exclaimed Joyce under her breath, turning surprised eyes upon Madame Bonnivel, as if that lady could meet her speaking glance.

And so she could in spirit, for her perceptions amounted almost to mind-reading. A smile of amusement lit up her sweet face, as she cried merrily,

"Father and daughter, are they? What a coincidence!"

Dalton looked from one to the other, uncomprehending.

Then his gaze lingered on Joyce's flushing cheek. As she made no effort to explain he said, presently, "I thought Mrs. Bonnivel might like some refreshments, and I told Mr. Driscoll, if he would take his wife and sister I would come for you two ladies. But he said they had gone home with the baby."

"Have they? And what has become of Mrs. Phelps?" asked Joyce, feeling somewhat forsaken by her clan.

"She went in with the doctor some time ago. I rather think she has left, too. She had a headache, or something."

Joyce glanced around her with a dissatisfied expression.

"No," she said, "this won't do! We might as well all have stayed at home as to come here just for a supercilious glance or two, while we huddle together. And yet—whom can I ask to take me?"

Dalton, with his eyes upon her, wondered. Had she been at a ball, among her own kind, who would not have wanted her? Even had no hint of possessions gone abroad, she was peerless in beauty and brightness. He made a queer little sound which Madame caught, and laughed softly.

"You could ask anybody to take *me*," she said with evident amusement, "and possibly, if Mr. Dalton tries hard, he may find somebody even to take you, Joyce. I scarcely think they would refuse him."

He evidently appreciated her fine sarcasm.

"I could try hard," he returned, "provided I am too good for the office, myself. Let me see. I suppose Miss Lavillotte will not be satisfied unless I bring somebody as unattractive as possible—wait, I have it!"

With a quick "Excuse me!" he hurried away, soon to return with a grizzled man of uncertain age, who certainly was not attractive, though so greatly improved by clean linen and a stiff collar that Dalton had noticed the change at once. He was, in fact, the very man whom Dan so often heard haranguing in the cobbler's shop, and knew as Tonguey Murfree, though when voting he registered as Joseph H.

With an air of exaggerated courtesy Dalton led him up and introduced him.

"Mrs. Bonnivel, Miss Lavillotte, let me present Mr. Murfree, well known of all in Littleton because of his eloquence. I'm sure he will be glad to take you out to supper, and give you his latest views on—well, say anarchy."

The man winced a little, and his florid face took on an added color. In his embarrassment he giggled like a bashful boy, and scraped one foot behind him in a low obeisance.

"Glad to please the lady, I'm sure," he muttered, quite at his wits' end what to do next.

Joyce rather resented the hint of derision in all this, and stepping forth a bit proudly, said at once,

"Thank you. If you'll just pilot me through to the refreshment room, Mr. Murfree—that is, if you know the way."

"Bet I do, 'm, and had a taste and sup myself, but I'm not backward to go again. The coffee's rare good, 'm, an the san'wiches very satisfying. But"—in a confidential tone, as they moved slowly through the throng—"whoever's a-doing of all this has made one big mistake, ma'am, and that's a fact."

"Indeed! How is that?"

"Well, it's on the drinks, 'm. He might at least have give us ginger-beer, or pop, if he's teetotal, as they say. It 'ud seem more nateral, somehow, to be drinking stuff outen a glass. But take it all together it's a pretty decent show, and the pictures and funnygraph, up in the big room, was fine. But if it's jest a scheme to play some new game on us they needn't try it. We've got our eyes peeled, and we don't get tooken in again. Old Early played it up pretty cute once, or twice, and we bit like suckers, only to wake up with a strong hook in our gills; but this young feller hasn't got the old one's experyunce, and he'll make a mess of it, if he tries any dodges. You jest set that down, 'fore you forgit it!"

"I don't see what dodge there can be in opening a pleasant house to you and giving you a nice party," returned Joyce, trying to keep her tone free of resentment.

"Oh well, we can't tell, yet. But maybe you ain't heard that they're going to have fees, and tax the liquors, and all that? Well, I have, and I say 'tain't fair, and he'd better not try it on us! We know our rights, and we're going to have 'em."

He made a flourish with his hands that nearly knocked the hat from a girl in the path they were slowly treading, and the young owner turned suddenly. It was Lucy Hapgood.

"Look out there, you"—she began, then catching sight of Joyce she blushed a little, ducked a courtesy, and turned once more to the man.

"What's the matter with you now, Tonguey Murfree? Ain't this good enough for you? You'd blow if you was in a palace, sitting on a throne, I do believe. You'd find some trick about it, some'ers."

Joyce met her laughing eyes and felt a hearty liking for her.

"You and I aren't looking for tricks, are we?" she said. "Have you had a good time?"

"Boss! and I hate to go, but I ought to, 'cause poor Nate'll be sleepy, and he has to get to work early mornings. He stayed with the young 'uns for me."

"And you have seen everything, Lucy?"

"Guess I didn't miss much," laughing happily, "My! but the supper was good. I only wished I could eat more, or else take some of it home. I ain't much on the cooking yet."

"You'll soon learn," encouraged Joyce. "How would you enjoy joining a cooking class, and learning how to do it all?"

The girl's honest gray eyes twinkled under the the long dark lashes, which gave them such pretty shadows.

"Would they let you sample the truck they cooked? Guess I could stand it, then! But I don't get much time for folderols."

Joyce saw that her escort was uneasy at the delay, so said

good-night cheerily and followed him. But her fastidious ideas received a shock at the scene which met them before the refreshment-rooms. Two of the parlors had been fitted up with chairs, ranged closely around the walls, and a table heaped with cups and plates, in the center. About sixty could be accommodated in each, but three times that number were scrambling for admittance outside.

The attendants appointed at these doors seemed powerless to keep order, and Larry had planted himself before one and was trying to pacify the hungry crowd, and promote harmony. For the shoving, pushing and swearing were not all good-natured, though largely so.

"Hold on there!" he called to a bull-headed Pole, who had just thrust aside a little girl so roughly she cried out with pain, "Hold on! There's enough to eat, and time enough to eat it in, but nobody gets inside here unless he brings his manners with him. This isn't pay-day, nor the menagerie, nor a bread riot; it's just a party of ladies and gentlemen, and we've all got to brace up and remember it. Ladies first, now, and stand aside there to let these folks out, or there can't anybody get in. No hurry! No hurry! the cooks will keep the coffee hot, and the sandwiches haven't even begun to give out. Hello, Joyce! Do you want to come now?"

"No, no, we'll wait," nodding gaily. "Let these others in who have waited longer."

The Pole turned to look at her, while he stood stolidly in the path, as close to the door as he could crowd, and his expression startled her. The gaunt eyes gleamed like those of a wolf, and over the high bones above the sunken cheeks the skin glistened, as if so tightly stretched as to be in danger of bursting. She felt that the man had been in desperate straits, and while recoiling before the evil sullenness of his look, she felt a deep pity for the pain in it. She turned to Murfree. "Who is that?" she had it on her tongue's end to ask, but the look in his face drove the query out of her mind. With hands clenched at his side, eyes staring through his glasses, and lips curled fiercely back from his set teeth, yellowed horribly with tobacco, the man was also gazing at the Pole, too intent to remember her presence.

CHAPTER XIII

SOME ENCOUNTERS

Joyce watched him a moment, fascinated. Presently he drew a long breath, and the tense features relaxed. He seemed gathering himself, together, and after a short interval of silence, during which she pretended to be absorbed in the crowd which was streaming through the door, he said in a low, husky voice:

"Say 'm, if you don't mind, and seeing's your ma is right here"—he referred to Madame Bonnivel who was slowly approaching on Mr. Dalton's arm—"I guess I'd better git out o' this crowd and go home, I ain't feeling very well and—good-night!"

He slipped aside without more ado, ducked his shock head, and, before she had time to collect her surprised senses, had melted away in the thinning swirls of humanity, and was gone.

"What! Deserted already?" laughed Mr. Dalton with malicious satisfaction, as he caught the expression on her face; but, softening instantly, he added, "Well, you're lucky! What I had expected was that you would never be rid of him till he had talked you bl—" He checked the word on his lips, remembering, his companion's affliction.

She laughed out merrily.

"How can one talk another blind? We should say deaf, I think. The blind always enjoy the merry clatter of tongues. Why did he leave, Joyce?"

"I don't just understand. He didn't feel well, he said."

"Oh, you overpowered him, Miss Lavillotte! He is not used to beauty and grandeur. I am a little afraid of it myself!" His own audacity, which surprised himself it was so unlike him, made George Dalton color like a girl, and he fairly shrank behind the Madame's tall figure to conceal his rising color. But Joyce did not notice. She was so intent on what she had just seen, as to be oblivious now. She took the dear lady's arm with a delightful sense of security, and observed in as matter-of-fact a way as she could assume:

"We'll have to wait, anyhow, for the people seem actually ravenous, poor things! I drew back to let them by, and thought we would go home—"

"No, you can come," cried Larry, bustling up to them. "Everybody is seated and I've found some extra chairs and a retired corner for you ladies, where you can see without being seen. Dalton and I will wait on you. Follow me."

He led them across a screened corner and seated them within one of the eating-rooms, nearly hidden behind the well-heaped table, which had been pushed back into an angle of the wall. As Joyce looked about her the Pole was nearly opposite, and sat gorging the large sandwich, handed him upon his plate, in a greedy manner that fairly horrified her. There was something animal-like, ghoulish even, in his clutching haste; yet it was pitiable, too.

"Mr. Dalton," she asked, "who is that man?"

He followed the guarded glance of her eye and looked a moment with a perplexed frown.

"I really can't tell," he said at length. "Yet it seems as if I ought to know, too. I hardly think he's one of our men, unless he has come very lately. He isn't exactly what you'd call a beauty; is he, Miss Lavillotte?"

"Far from it. He looks as if he had suffered awfully, don't you think?"

"Oh possibly—suffering, or sin—one can scarcely tell which it may be at a glance. I'll step and get you the cream and sugar, Mrs. Bonnivel."

Joyce continued to watch the man furtively, neglecting her own food. Every time the sandwiches went by he snatched at them, gulping down his coffee, between whiles, in great hot swallows that made his dreadful eyes stand out still more than was natural. Used as the attendants were to irregularities in this non-etiquetical company, they showed their disgust plainly at his boorishness. Two of them stopped a moment near Joyce's corner, to discuss him in no measured terms. One said,

"Not another thing does he get here, the brute! If he thinks we're keeping a free lunch counter for the likes of him he's mistaken. He hasn't got common decency."

Joyce saw him clear the last crumb from his plate, and glance furtively to and fro from under his bent brows, with a movement that filled her with disgust and pity.

"The poor wretch is starving!" she thought. "The sight and smell of food drive him wild. Where can he have been?"

Even as she was thinking this there was a general movement, and he too rose from his place with the rest. Cup in hand, he neared the table as if to deposit it there before leaving; but his eyes were on a half-emptied tray of the sandwiches just placed there, and as he stooped to set down the cup he made a quick movement, and scooped up a little heap of the slices into the hollow of his hands, from which they slid into a coat pocket with dextrous suddenness. Some one stepped forward with an exclamation at which, with one bound, he sprang between the Madame and Joyce, dodged behind the screen, and when the attendant reached it, had disappeared. The latter turned back with a crestfallen air.

"Did you see that?" he cried excitedly. "I never saw such a hog!"

Joyce rose, and touched him lightly on the arm.

"I think it's hardly worth making a fuss about," she said gently. "He seemed very hungry—starving, indeed. There's plenty of everything, isn't there?"

"Oh, yes, but it makes me mad to be so imposed on! I don't believe the fellow belongs here, anyhow."

"He looked like a sailor to me," she observed thoughtfully.

"Umph! Like a jail-bird I should say, Miss. Will I bring you some more coffee now?"

"No, nothing more, thank you. Just kindly take my cup."

Larry came up to them, wiping the perspiration from his brow.

Fannie E. Newberry

"Whew! but I'm used up. Aren't you ready to go home, mother? And you Joyce—do you want to stay all night? If I can once get you safely out of this, I shall be glad!"

"Safely out—why do you speak like that, Larry?"

"Then you haven't heard anything here?" looking from one to the other, surprisedly.

"Nothing save what you are hearing now, the clatter of many tongues and plates. Why, my son?"

"Oh! nothing, only there has just been a pretty sharp scrimmage outside. That ugly-looking fellow I had to rebuke for rudeness, out here, was pushing his way to the outer door in the way he seems to affect, when he ran plump into an old party—let's see, they said his name was Murphy, I think, or something like that—and of a sudden—well! they sprang at each others' throats like a couple of tigers. They were right in the midst of it, and every one too astonished to move, when in came a couple of the city police, gave one look, and in a trice had my ugly man thrown down and were putting on the bracelets. It seems, the fellow's an escaped convict, and has been hiding around here in the woods for weeks. He must have been so nearly starved as to lose all caution before coming to so public a place. I can't understand it, myself, but I presume he would have escaped unmolested, only for the fight. Dalton," turning to the manager who had just returned from his prolonged absence, "what does it all mean, anyhow? I suppose you saw the fracas?"

"No, I got there just as it was all over, and I can't tell you much about it. They've taken the man away, and Murfree, too. The latter is pretty badly used up and can't talk. That was as savage a brute as I ever saw!"

"He was a desperate man," said Joyce, still feeling the stirrings of pity. "He was nearly starved to death, and there was something awful between him and that Murfree—I could see that."

"You could?" The manager gave her a wondering glance.

"Are you very observing? No one seems to know any reason for his springing upon Murfree so."

"There *was* a reason," persisted Joyce. "They had met before, I'm certain. Come, ma mere, let's go home."

"You are tired, child. Yes, we will go at once. It must be late."

Joyce's tone had expressed more than weariness, and Madame Bonnivel's heart ached for her disappointment and chagrin. She took the girl's hand and drew her along.

"Larry, you'll stay with Mr. Dalton and help preserve order! Gilbert can accompany us."

"Oh, if I must," shrugging his shoulders. "But I feel that a motion for all to adjourn would be in order; don't you, Dalton?"

"All right! We'll clear the rooms in no time."

Joyce stopped him with an uplifted hand.

"They must go when and as they choose. It is *their* party. Please don't interfere in the least. Come Madame, we can slip out unnoticed. Nobody needs us here."

The two stepped briskly on, and Dalton, watching Joyce,

shook his head ruefully, then turned to Larry.

"It's too bad she's just as she is. It means a lot of heartbreaks and disappointments. Pity women can't take the world as it is."

"Well, perhaps—provided they don't leave it as it is. I am inclined to believe it's that kind of woman who is responsible for the fact that the world does grow better as the centuries pass. And those who know Joyce Lavillotte would scarcely care to change her."

"No, no; nor I! It was of herself I was thinking. She's got to suffer so. One hates to see a person take a cloud for something tangible and keep falling off, to be bruised and beaten. If she could always soar—but the falls will come."

He sighed, and Larry laughed.

"She'd rather bear the falls than never soar. Let her alone!"

"Oh, of course; it's all one can do. But—it hurts."

The last words were in a whisper, so lost on Larry, who had just turned to speak with the phonograph exhibitor now making ready to depart.

Meanwhile, the Madame and Joyce had hastily gathered up their wraps, and were waiting an instant in the hall till Gilbert could make his way to them from the corner out of which they had beckoned him, (nothing loth, for he was half asleep,) when Rachel passed them quickly, her own wrap on her arm. She looked flushed and animated. Her cold, indifferent mask seemed to have fallen from her face. Her mother was awaiting her, the sleeping baby folded in her shawl.

"Well, d'ye have a good time?" she asked, as the daughter

joined her.

"So good I can hardly believe it's real, mother!" was the glad answer. Then, catching sight of the ladies near by, she bowed slightly, with a shy smile at Joyce.

"Good-night," she said softly, flushing a little. "Are you going, too? It's been fine, hasn't it?"

In her surprised pleasure Joyce forgot to answer, except with a vigorous nod and smile, but in an instant she whispered in a brightening tone, "It was Rachel, ma mere. Did you hear?"

"Yes, I did. I could hear the joy in her tone, too. It has been a good time for many, I know, and gladness will soften the hardest and coldest, Joyce. Don't falter because wrong must still be, daughter. People have to be educated in enjoyment as well as in anything else. It may not be one of the first, or best, things in life, but it has its uses, and they are many. My Joyce is not working for appreciation, nor for praise, but just to better these who have become peculiarly her own people. Let us be patient, dear."

And Joyce, though bruised and worn, was not quite beaten, though the evening had been so far from realizing her anticipations. Lucy and Rachel had been pleased, at least. That was something!

Fannie E. Newberry

CHAPTER XIV

JOYCE AND HER MANAGER

"In *every* house, Miss Lavillotte? Beg pardon, but have you considered the cost?" Mr. Dalton wore his business face, with its sternest expression, and it did not relent even when he looked up into hers.

Joyce smiled in spite of it, and fished out a newspaper-clipping from her plethoric pocket-book, which she handed her manager with a ceremonious air. He read it, and his visage grew perplexed and miserable.

"M-mm, 'grand entertainment. Five hundred for flowers. Gown of hostess embroidered in seed pearls. Jewels a thousand, and at least ten'—are you sure this is what you meant me to read? You know it's all Greek to me!" looking down with deprecation into her laughing, upturned eyes.

"Perfectly sure. You see who gave that entertainment?"

"Yes, I see."

"Is she a richer woman than I? Has she a larger income?"

"About the same, I presume."

"And the expenses she incurred, as detailed there, were for one evening?"

"Yes. Doubtless this is greatly exaggerated, though. These news items about swelldom usually are, aren't they?"

"I cannot tell, not belonging to swelldom, myself. But granting all that, and allowing even half off, if you say so, it will still exceed what this plan is to cost me. And my little fun is not for one lone evening, but for a whole year, in which nearly five hundred people will share and be benefited—not simply amused or bored."

"You are good at arguing, Miss Lavillotte, and your money is your own. If you wish to squander it that way"—He stopped abruptly, warned by the flash of her eye.

"I had not used that word in this connection," she said coldly, "but you may if you choose."

"Well," he returned, in some desperation, "we'll drop the word 'squander,' then, if it is offensive to you. But you must allow you are spending a great deal, mustn't you? Some of it is well spent, I'll admit, and—and it's none of my business at all—but when it comes to telephones and for those people— please don't be angry, Miss Lavillotte!—it does seem absurd."

Joyce laughed good-naturedly. His distress was genuine.

"I know it must from your point of view, but now pray listen to mine. I believe that there are certain essentials of easy living that ought to be practically free to all, and might be, if managed correctly. Of these, four are air and water, light and heat, and the fifth is prompt communication with your fellow-men. When my grandmother was a girl it cost a neat

Fannie E. Newberry

little sum to send a letter anywhere, and hundreds of families, unable to bear the expense of correspondence, lost sight of each other, often for years, sometimes for life, in the unavoidable separation which must come to all growing households. After a time this matter appealed so strongly to thinking men that they decided to make a great national matter of it, and they established a wonderful mail service, and have kept lowering the rates and adding to the perfection of the service, until now hardly any one is so poor he cannot write a line to a friend, if only on a postal card. Now a quicker, better means of communication is given us in the telephone and telegraph, and I claim that these should also be regulated and run by government in the interests of the people, and thus made available to all at nominal rates. I can't control Congress, but I can control Littleton with its few hundred souls, and that I mean to do in this. Every house shall have its 'phone, that every person may have the opportunity to express his wants at once, or to call in help, if needed."

Dalton gave a hopeless shrug.

"They'll use them for gossiping, mostly."

"No, that is to be regulated. The time allowed for each separate use will be short, and if any abuse the privilege they will be cut off."

"Humph! Do you expect one central to manage it all?"

"Yes, one officer, but not one girl. I shall have four people, all told, two girls for day hours and two men for night hours. I intend to have them work in relays—four hours off and four on. It is too nervous a strain for longer hours than that. The night operators will have a cot for the one off duty, so that if anything unusual happens the waking one can call the other. I think it must be doleful to stay alone in such a place during those gruesome night hours. I couldn't have it at all."

Dalton laughed outright.

"Positively, Miss Lavillotte, you are too funny! Do you expect to do away with everything disagreeable in your model village?"

"I wish I could, but I do not hope for that. Disagreeable people, who oppose one in everything, will always exist, I fear." Her tone was innocently sad. "But I do mean to try and eradicate what is unnecessarily disagreeable, if scheming can do it. And now, if you are through laughing, Mr. Dalton, I will tell you how I propose to pay for this telephone service without feeling it so severely as you seem to think I shall."

"I am listening, madam."

"Well, I have made a contract, only awaiting your approval and signature, to furnish the glass insulators and the jars, so many thousand a year—wait! I have the figures here somewhere. I never could remember figures—ah! here it is—in exchange."

"You have? Well, I declare! You really do show aptitude for business, I'll have to own."

"Don't I?" laughing with as much pleasure as a child that has turned scolding into praise. "I'm delighted about it in more ways than one. It will give employment to our unskilled hands, who are now idle half the time. Even the children can turn a penny on their holidays, if they like."

Dalton caught at the paper and looked it over with careful scrutiny, his face lighting as he gazed.

"Really!" he said at length, glancing up to give her an approving nod, "really, this isn't bad—that is, I mean you have made a good bargain, for all I can see, and given us the opportunity to work up a new line that may prove lucrative. I wouldn't have thought it of a girl—a young lady like you."

She laughed amusedly.

"I'm glad I have been able to please you at last, Mr. Dalton! The electricians will begin wiring the town in a few days. They will put in a cheap style of 'phone, as it is not looks we are after but convenience, and will hurry the work right through." She stopped with some hesitation of manner, but looked as if more was to come, and her manager gave her a respectful, questioning glance.

"There's another thing," she said presently in a rather faint voice, "the central office is also to be an exchange."

"A—what?"

"An exchange. You see, that's really my main reason for having the 'phones. I want my people to learn what the one right principle of exchange is. We talk about money being the medium of exchange, and as such it is thought to be the best thing on earth. Yet the greed of it is the root of all evil. I want to come back to first principles a little, and exchange from man to man, without this pernicious medium that has filled us with covetousness and a lack of consideration for others. I want to see if people are really so callous and cold to each other as they seem, or if this unreadiness to help is only because we are too greatly separated by the many mediums interposed—which prove barriers instead of channels. I want to find if every need cannot somehow, somewhere, meet its fulfilment, unless death itself has shut out the way. It is too limited a field, here, to learn absolutely, but it may give us some idea, and then—"

Mr. Dalton had settled back into his chair with a non-committal expression, and was drumming on the desk before him.

"I'm afraid," he murmured in a concise tone, "that you are talking above my head."

Joyce, rudely aroused from her introspective vision, looked at him rather blankly a moment, then sprang to her feet. At first she seemed offended, then cried briskly, with a mischievous air,

"And through my hat? I know that is what you wanted to say! Well, never mind. Some people hunt for north poles, some for new continents in the tropics, some are content with finding an unclassified species of bug. I want to experiment with human needs and longings a bit. It is my fad just now. You know fads are fashionable."

"Miss Lavillotte, did any one ever tell you that you are a despot?"

"I?" Joyce's eyes opened their widest, "I a despot!"

"Yes. You want to rule as absolutely as any Czar; but not only that; you want to play the part of Providence, and watch the workings of your will—"

"Stop! Mr. Barrington said that, and I told him I wanted my people to play that part to each other. And I am right. It was the teaching of Christ. 'Do it in My name'—surely it *is* right! Mr. Dalton, it is unfair, even ridiculous, if I may so speak, to lay all our mistakes and misdemeanors at the door of our Creator. He gives us sense, reason, patience, ingenuity. What are they for? To be hidden in a napkin till some crushing calamity comes and shakes us out of our indifference enough to make us exercise them? No! They are given us to prevent calamity, to wrest from earth, air, and sea what is needed for our comfort. He gave man *dominion*. That does not mean just sitting back and bearing with resignation. It means using every faculty to reduce contending forces to our requirements. Patience is not half a virtue when it simply implies an uncomplaining endurance because one thinks he must endure. The patience that will *not* endure, but tries and tries again to rectify the ill is the best patience. It never turns aside, never lays down its tools, always has a new plan when the old is crushed out—that is the real patience! You call me a despot—you are unjust! It is only that you don't understand, I do not want to rule for the sake of power, but because people are so supine they will not learn to rule without being pushed into it. I do want to learn to shape circumstances, but not to control Littleton. I do wish to teach them what self-government really means, though. And see how I am placed. Here is this great fortune which I will not use for myself partly because my needs are simple, partly because—well, because I won't. Thus I am given an opportunity few can have. Many have my ideas without the money; a few have the money without the ideas. It happens I have both, and I mean to try for myself whether it is not possible for a community to live on little money and yet have the comforts—yes, even what some consider the luxuries— of life, simply through perfect co-operation, swift communication, and a governing power that is centered in their wishes for their best good."

She stopped abruptly and put her palms to her face with a child-like movement. Her cheeks were hot and flushed.

"How silly to get so excited! You will question my plans with reason if I cannot keep my head in argument."

"One has to question till one can thoroughly understand. These are thoughts I have never gone into, Miss Lavillotte, I have been in danger of forgetting that there was anything more in life than just money-making. Will you tell me more, some day?"

His humble tone melted Joyce.

"Any time you like. And you know, Mr. Dalton, you are the real manager of it all. I shall have to look to you for the practical application of my possibly unpractical ideas. When I soar too high you must jerk me down to level ground."

"I begin to think I might like a cloud-ride myself occasionally, just for variety's sake," he laughed. "And I'll do whatever you tell me to, Miss Lavillotte," he added stoutly. "If the Works go to the dogs, all right, but you shall be obeyed! Only—may I ask a question?"

"Certainly."

"Have you put something safely away for your future where it can't be affected by things here?"

"Have I? Certainly not! Do you think I would make myself safe and sure when I might be wrecking so many? No, but unfortunately, on my mother's side, they are cautious. My great-uncle takes care of the right I have there, and I have never been allowed to meddle with it. He sends me two hundred dollars a month, and this is all I need for my living."

"Do you mean?"—His expressive glance swept her well-dressed person and she raised her hand protestingly.

"Don't ask too many questions!" she laughed. "Ellen used to be in a great modiste's establishment and knows the tricks of

Fannie E. Newberry

the trade. My dress and table cost me less a year than most women of means spend in a month. But good-by—oh! I forgot to say, Marie Sauzay is to be one of the telephone girls."

"Marie? The cripple?"

"Yes, she will go to and fro on a tricycle chair, and can thus eke out her sister's earnings. The knowledge that she can do this will almost make her well, I know. She is so ambitious! A messenger has been negotiating with her and told me of her delight in the prospects. The other girl will be a trained one sent by the company. Will you select my night men? They must be sober fellows—possibly somebody can be found who is not good in the Works."

"I'll see to it, and, Miss Lavillotte—"

"Well?"

"Who put all these ideas into your head, please? You are so young!"

She smiled, while blushing deeply.

"Won't you give me any credit for originality, Mr. Dalton? How can one tell where one picks up ideas? They are like pebbles in our pathway; sometimes we never even see them, but carelessly scuff them aside as we walk. Then the sun of somebody's genius shines out and shows them to be gems, and we hasten to pick them up and claim them for our own. I have been taught when to watch for the sun's shining—that's all!"

She waved her hand, nodded, and hurried out of the office, leaving Dalton gazing after her with an eager, baffled face.

CHAPTER XV

MOTHER FLAHERTY'S TELEPHONE

There was great merriment in Littleton over the advent of the
telephone. The women gossips gathered with their babies in
their arms and even the men (whom no one would venture
thus to name) smoked and stood about in groups during all
the long summer evenings, to discuss this latest marvel.
Among them, with many differences of opinion, there was
much laughter and disclaiming. Old Mrs. Flaherty declared,
amid her giggles, that "the two eyes av the craythur fairly
give her a turn," and when asked to explain she pointed to
the gongs at the top of the apparatus. Lucy Hapgood had
heard of live wires, and shrank from touching even the
receiver till repeatedly assured there was no danger of
electrocution. And when at last she did consent to put it to
her ear, and heard her father calling to her from Cole's
grocery, she shrieked with astonished awe. For the telephone
was as little known in this hamlet as if it had been situated a
thousand miles from the metropolis, instead of less than two-
score. The limitations of poverty are great, and even fifty-
cent fares to the city were seldom compassed, except where,
possibly, a legal holiday and a wedding fell on the same day,
and the occasion was made memorable by an outing. Even
then the returned travelers would have little to relate, except
such scenes as clustered around the great depot with its

neighboring lodging-houses and saloons. Of parks, galleries, museums, libraries, and palatial dwellings, these tourists scarcely dreamed, and never thought to visit. All dread those things they do not understand, and these people would have told you they had no wish to see such places; they were out of their line.

So all of the older and more conservative Littletonians looked with open disfavor upon the new "speaking machines," and some absolutely refused to use them. In fact, a few did not hesitate to say such doings smacked of the evil one, and one old dame set her sudsy arms akimbo and stoutly defied the electricians to enter her house.

"You kin string up them wires from here to Jerichy, if you want to," she said sternly, letting her lance-like eyes rove in scornful leisure over their equipment, "but you can't bring 'em inside my dure. No, sir! I don't want any voices rousin' me up at all hours of the day an' night. If folks at 'tother end o' town wants to speak to me they knows where to find me. I'm a respictable widdy lady what keeps to home and minds my own washin', and they can't no man nor woman, nuther, get a chance to sass me through any mash-ine. No, sir! I know that young Early. He's got a scheme to see all thet's a-goin' on amongst us day and night, and I won't have it. Tain't decent, and they ain't no law on his side. So jest git along with you now, and don't take up my time a-wranglin', for I've got work to do, if you haven't."

The men, who had stood in dazed silence, looking sheepishly at each other, went meekly on their way, and one home, at least, boasted no telephone. Indeed, to establish that exchange which was Joyce's dream, seemed for a time a ridiculous failure. The attempt to make these people understand that only good was intended them seemed positively useless. When it was again and again reiterated, by means of printed dodgers shed broadcast among the homes, by Dalton's talks to the boys in the factory at the closing hour, even by Marie Sauzey's urgings over the wire from the central office, that every stringent need, or helpful offer, was to be communicated to her by telephone, they simply winked at each other, and, hanging up the receiver, whispered to any who happened to be present,

"Didn't I tell you, now? It's spies they are, and nothin' else. Sorra a word do they get out o' me this day!"

But one morning, poor old Mother Flaherty suffered a sad accident when quite alone in her cottage. Trying to balance herself on an uncertain chair, in her effort to reach a bottle of medicine on the top shelf of her cupboard, her rickety support gave way and let her down with cruel celerity. Her poor old bones were brittle and snapped with the concussion. When she tried to raise herself, after her momentary groans and exclamations, she found it impossible, for the left femur was broken. She wavered for a time between spells of semi-consciousness, and rousings to fresh shrieks and wails, the pain growing momently more agonizing and the floor more intolerable in its cold and hardness. But the shouts of some children out at play drowned her feeble old voice in happier sounds, and no one heard. She had given herself up to a lonely, horrible death when her wild, roving gaze fell upon the telephone not three feet away, and she remembered the oft-repeated injunction to tell her wants into its non-committal ear. She had no faith in the thing, and was half-afraid of it, believing it a temptation of Satan, but the situation had become unbearable. Flesh weakened and spirit failed. She would try it as a last resort, then cross herself and die. Dragging herself painfully with groans and sobs, she managed to reach up with a broomstick and jog a faint ring out of the gong, at the same time shouting at it in a fury of horror and anxiety,

Fannie E. Newberry

"Help! Help! Help! I'm kilt intirely. I want a do-octhor!"

The confused sounds that reached Marie were vibrating with trouble and despair, but that long-drawn "do-octhor" came plainly enough for her to know what was needed, though she could get no response to her agitated questioning. She called Dr. Browne up at once, and sent him flying. Poor Mrs. Flaherty, meanwhile, had sunk back, almost spent with her painful exertion, thinking in her desolation,

"It's no good at all, at all! And now I must die unshriven, wid that awful sin on me sowl."

But suddenly the blissful clatter of a man's quick footsteps aroused her, and she saw, as in a vision, the door thrown wide, and the doctor's commiserating face bending above her. His outbreak, "Well, well, well, this *is* a fix!" sent comfort to her failing consciousness as, with a groan of relief, she slipped into blissful oblivion.

There was no time for talk that day, but when the old creature was resting in her cast, with her nerves soothed into quietude, the next, she looked up at her daughter, who had hurried to her bedside, and asked huskily,

"Norah, tell me thrue; was it the spakin'-mash-ine did it?"

"Did what, mother?"

"You know, don't yez? Did it bring the docthor?"

"Why, yes. When you called up the central, of course they 'phoned the doctor, and so—"

"Norah, will yez shtop thot gabblin', now? What does I be knowin' of centhrals, and all thot? Can't you answer plain, yis or no? Did the spakin'-mash-ine get me the docthor?"

"Yes, mother, it did."

"Thin I'm beholden to it. And I take back all me hard woords and thochts. Give me another sup o' thot cordial, now, till I go to slape. And ye may tell the neighbors, fur me, thot I've thried and I know yez can get what ye nade fur the askin' out o' thim mash-ines. Now be off wid yez—I'm going to slape."

Of course the word spread, and those who had been wise enough to say little in disfavor of the innovation plumed themselves upon their superior information, while the ranters against it were temporarily silenced. Joyce, who was burning with impatience over their slow acceptance of her benefits, fairly ached to go among them with vigorous exhortations, even commands, but the Madame restrained her.

"I wouldn't, Joyce," she said in her ruminant tone. "Let them find out things for themselves. It is the only true wisdom, and nobody wants even cake thrust down his throat. Try the Lord's way, child. We are slower in accepting His good gifts than these people are to believe in yours, yet He waits patiently, and in time we learn their worth."

One morning, however, soon after Mrs. Flaherty's accident, Joyce made an errand into the central office, and while waiting for some distant connection to be made ventured to ask some questions of Marie who, alert and bright-eyed, sat in her wheeled chair, so adjusted that the switch-board was within easy reach.

"You don't have much to do here, they tell me," she began, smiling at the little Frenchwoman in friendly fashion.

Marie now knew Miss Lavillotte as the resident on the knoll, who was popularly supposed to be interested in schools, possibly with the intention of teaching some day, and who had means enough to run a modest establishment of her own. She answered eagerly,

"But, yes, by times I do. It is the young people that do use it most, though. Dose old ones, they so mooch vork do all the day that they will not yet take time to learn so that it seem not strange to them. It will be otherwise in time."

"Do they tell their needs at all?" began Joyce, when Marie had to answer a call, and sat smiling in that way which seems meaningless to a looker-on while some one's voice holds the attention at the other end. Presently she answered in quick tones. "Yes, it is so indeed. I will make note, and see if it may have answer. Yes. Oh, but that is true! Yes. All right, Good-by."

Joyce longed, yet hesitated, to ask what the communication had been, when Marie turned to her.

"You but now did ask, 'Do they tell their needs?' and this was one."

"Really? What was it? Pray tell me! Could it be gratified? I'd so like to know."

Marie smiled at the eagerness of her visitor.

"I tell you, then. It was Mr. Gus Peters, who want somebody to make him one easel, with a drawing-board that will slide up and down easy, for one nice sharp knife with three blade that he will give in exchange. He laugh w'en he say it, as if he think it no use, though."

"But it ought to be of use. Let's think, Marie. Who can do

such things? Somebody that needs a nice knife. Some bright boy, say, with a head for such work."

Marie thought a minute.

"There is a boy," she said slowly. "He is not good for mooch, but he like that whittle kind of work, I know."

"Poor child! His mother, she is dead, and his father he have no time to be kind to him, I think, so he wander about and pick up the job here and there. It is he that might do this easel."

"Just the thing! Only he couldn't get the materials together, I fear—wait! Where does he live?"

"In a leetle house back behind of the Vorks, and a seester zat ees older do housekeep, I believe. She is—not good." Marie spoke reluctantly, and turned sad eyes upon Joyce.

"Oh! that is dreadful," cried the latter. "Perhaps—ah! a ring."

Marie was kept busy awhile, several calls succeeding each other rapidly.

"Ah! they do plan to make me confuse," she laughed presently, turning back to Joyce. "See! I have these demands, and they do all laugh as they say them. Lucie Hapgood, she desire a nice ribbon blue for her hat; Mrs. Myron, where a new baby is come, do want a somebody to sit wiz her zis afternoon, so her seester get a leetle rest! Joe Granger, whose vife is away, do long for one goot dinner zis noon and they do need for Mother Flaherty a chair which will raise and lower, zat she may rest from her bed."

"Dear me, it *is* a jumble!" laughed Joyce. "Well, let me help

Fannie E. Newberry

you out. Don't Lucy's children all go to school now, except the baby?"

"The leetle baby—yes."

"Then couldn't she take it over to Mrs. Myron's till school is out, and look after that lady, who perhaps would give her the blue ribbon to pay for the service? And ask Norah Flaherty if she won't let Joe Granger come there to dinner, if he will hunt up the chair for her mother—and send Joe to me for the chair. You will have to keep reminding them that an exchange means always giving something for what they get; and if I were you, Marie, when they began to tell of a want I should ask at once, "But what have you to give?" That is the important part. You see Gus Peters understood it."

"Yes, I see. And some one haf tell you all ze whole plan, I see too," returned Marie, looking at her somewhat wonderingly.

"Why, ye-s, I know about it, and it does interest me greatly. It's like a puzzle, somehow. Two and two may not always make four, but they will certainly make something. Do you mind my planning with you a little?"

"Not one bit, dear Mees."

"Then let's fix Gus Peters out. Why not phone to that boy— what's his name?"

"Wolly, zey call him zat ozzer name, it ees very deficult to speak and I forget."

"Oh well, Wolly will do. You know his number on the circuit?" Marie pointed it out and called up the house. Wolly was not there, but his sister seemed to think any job would be welcome. The only thing was, he had no tools and no lumber, neither had he money to buy them,

"Now, if some good person who haf ze lumbare would but need something," laughed Marie.

"Wait! I have it. Gus is an architect. There is a great deal of building being done. Possibly Gus could turn himself in some way to get the lumber for the boy."

"And gif the knife, too?"

"The work ought to be worth it. May I talk to Gus?"

"To be sure," giggling enjoyably, for the whole thing seemed a huge joke to the French girl, and even to Joyce it began to seem rather a complicated affair. She felt certain, still, that her principle was all right, but began to perceive that, even so, its practical working might be almost an impossibility.

"If I could always be on hand to adjust matters!" she thought inwardly. "But I can see that when they really begin to use their 'phones at all, as most owners of them do, this exchange business would become a rather unwieldy affair." Then Joyce sighed so profoundly that Gus heard it at the other end, even as he spoke his "Hello!"

A moment's talk with him adjusted that matter. He said readily enough that he could get the youngster what he needed without the least trouble—all he wanted was to be sure and get a decent working easel, and the knife would be forthcoming. So Joyce, relieved for the present, turned eagerly again to Marie.

"How about Lucy? Will Mrs. Myron give her the blue ribbon?"

"She ask eef peenk would rot do, and I say, talk wiz Lucie, and she do. Zat is ze way, of course. When one does say what one need we will say, 'try zo-and-zo,' and in time efery body will be serve, and eferybody happy."

"How quick you are to catch the idea, Marie! It will surely adjust itself as you get used to it. And oh! if it will work. If they can be taught—"

Joyce caught the other's astonished glance and checked herself instantly, annoyed enough that she had come so close to self-betrayal.

"You see how interested even I can get," she laughed, flushing with embarrassment. "It is silly of me, but it does seem such a novel scheme, and one that might help all without impoverishing any, if rightly used. I have really been anxious to watch its practical working. Thank you for letting me bother you so."

"'Tis no bodder. I like to see you always, Mees Lavillotte. Come often and again."

"I will be glad to. And, Marie, when you come to a dead-lock—do you know the meaning of that?—when you cannot fit any want with another want, as we have been doing now, just 'phone to me and perhaps I can help you. Never be afraid of asking for anything that is really needed. I have plenty of time, and such things interest me. And I have ways of getting things that make it easier than for some. You will remember this and surely call upon me?"

"It is verra good you do care," observed Marie, still a good bit amazed.

"You see I have chosen to make my home in Littleton, and I want to be one with you. I want to be helpful, as well as to get help."

"Zat ees a good way to feel. Littleton—zet ees our new name, I hear. It do sound strange to me yet. We nevare haf a name before. It was just the Vorks."

"Do you like the name?"

"Eh, what matters?" flinging out her hands in a way that proved her Parisian blood and birth. "It will do as well as any other, Littleton—Lavillotte—How strange that your name does mean 'the little town,' also! Did you know?"

"Does it?" Joyce felt it was time to flee. This Frenchwoman was too keen to be easily answered. She nodded brightly, perhaps at the question, perhaps to say adieu, and crying back over her shoulder, "Remember my request!" hurried away, laughing within herself at her narrow escape.

CHAPTER XVI

ON A TRAIL

Dan Price was not a guest either opening night at the social house. On the contrary, the first evening, the events of which have been related, he took his dinner pail and tackle, and despite the somewhat showery state of the atmosphere, pedaled out of the settlement towards his woodland haunt as fast as will and muscle could carry him. He had a supreme contempt for all these new "notions" at the Works, which he looked upon as the somewhat crazy hobbies of a man too young to realize what they meant, and too rich to care how he squandered his money. He knew that to go back to the old ways, after a taste of the new, would make that state of slavery seven times worse than before. Better let them alone in what they had become used to; and, for his own part, he wanted no patronizing, he told himself, nor anybody laying down the law as to how he should spend his leisure, either. Out of hours he was his own master, at least, and nobody need interfere. There were things in life worse than physical hardships—experience had sternly taught him that.

He would scarcely fling a glance in the direction of the well-lighted building, towards which already the younger tide of humanity was setting, and his dark face took on a sneer when he noted their evident excitement over the event.

"Always caught with something new!" he muttered to himself. "One would think it more decent to give up hoping sometime, but they never seem to. Haven't we been cheated with fair promises year after year—promises that were as empty as a glass bulb? And yet they all bite just as readily as ever. Even the chronic grumblers, like Murfree, Hapgood, and that gang, are beginning to come over. It makes me tired!"

As he reached a certain cottage he pedaled faster than ever, and with his head bent nearly to the handle-bars, flew by without a glance, or pause. Yet, without looking, he had discerned Rachel standing on the new square porch, exceptionally trim and stiff in a light muslin, while the children swarmed about her admiringly. He could also hear Mrs. Hemphill, from indoors somewhere, screaming her commands to the scattered family in a high key, though no one seemed paying the slightest attention. Had he been able to see out of the back of his head, as they say some women can do, he would have discovered that the smile died out of Rachel's face as he whizzed by, that she gazed after him a moment with a sober look, then turned and went into the house, answering her mother's remarks with a sharp,

"Well, what is it?"

Dan, meanwhile, tore ahead, leaving all artificial lights behind him, and sighed with relief when loneliness wrapped him around, so that he might relax a bit and take a long breath, for he was weary.

It was still far from being really dark, though dusky in the shadows, and, as he was wading the brook, something that was not a shadow seemed to move amid the darker smudges of the vine tangles and underbrush surrounding his little bower. He stopped splashing and peered intently, but saw nothing to confirm the impression and concluded it was but the waving of a branch, or the leap of a squirrel from bough to bough. But no sooner had he stepped foot on the soil than he saw someone had been here since his last visit, at least three weeks before. Vines had been torn down so that the entrance was visible, there were traces of a camp-fire on the sands at his feet, and he could see broken tree-twigs and limbs scattered about, as if in preparation for another. A chill crept over him at thought of this intrusion, and he looked around, half fearfully, as if expecting that someone might spring out from the deeper wood and dispute possession with him.

Keeping an anxious lookout to sides and rear he hastily entered the little leaf-tent, and saw, with a sort of despair, that it had been occupied. He almost groaned to see the scattered leaves from his bed in the corner, but was somewhat consoled to find that evidently no one had discovered the opening below.

"Some tramp," he thought. "It's queer they should find this place, so entirely off their routes, though. I wonder if that was the brute I saw skipping out, then? I've a notion to hunt him down. He's spoiled my rest for to-night, anyhow. And I never can feel safe again till I know who it was, and what it wanted."

But the possession of his wheel hampered him. He did not like to leave it, perhaps to be stolen, and it would be almost impossible to make his way through the brush with it. In a quandary he stepped forth again, to stand an instant among the over-hanging vines, making up his mind. He was so placed as to be invisible from the brookside, though he could see it plainly through the vine's interstices, and in that instant there saw a flash of something black against the vista of light, and he knew, rather than saw, that a man had leaped across the brook where it narrowed suddenly, further down.

The spray of the up-leaping water, as he jumped short, sparkled in the pale rays of a rising moon.

At this his resolution was formed. The man, whoever he was, had evidently headed for town. Dan decided instantly, to cross the brook higher up, at another narrow spot, take to the road, mount his wheel, and ride by this piece of woods as if with no object in view, then, when well ahead, hide in some good place and intercept him—or at least see who he might be. It did not take him long to recover the road, mount his wheel, and start. Nobody was yet in sight, but he had not expected to see anybody. The tramp would doubtless skulk along behind the fences till sure Dan was gone, then come out and trudge after as fast as possible. Such was the program the young man mapped out for him, at least. Once, as he toiled through a sandy reach, he was sure he saw the fellow skulking behind a rail fence, but he whistled negligently as he sprinted by and did not seem to notice, though the perspiration started a little at thought that this might be a desperate character, on his very heels, and well armed.

He kept up his pace, anxious to get to a certain spot he had fixed upon as his point of lookout. He presently reached it and, slowing up, gazed well about him. Nobody was in sight, and dusk was now real darkness. Still the moon, when not obscured by clouds, shone brightly. Just now their veil was thick, and a slight shower was beginning to fall. If these should part, any one crossing the road before him would show clearly against the sky.

He dismounted, hid his wheel behind a thick growth of untrimmed poplar saplings, and made himself comfortable in the dry bed of a ditch which crossed the road and was bridged over with a few planks. In the shadow cast by this bridge he crouched and, leaning against a boulder, settled himself for patient waiting. A great bull-frog, which had

Fannie E. Newberry

dropped out of sight at his approach, soon returned again, and croaked hoarsely of his personal affairs. For, in wet weather, this was a marshy spot, and he remembered happier days. Presently the clouds parted and the moon sent a brilliant spear shaft through the rent, making it almost like day. A startled peewit cried out, from his nest under the planking, that he had overslept, but was calmed into drowsiness by his wife's assuring tones; and a noisy beetle of some kind boomed and buzzed around, as if intoxicated by the very thought of daylight. Listening intently, amid all this soft murmur of sound, Dan presently began to hear afar the rhythmic beat of footsteps, falling hard and fast upon the beaten soil. His man was approaching.

He gathered himself together and slowly rose, creeping close to the wooden buttress of the bridge and staying well in its shadow. The footsteps grew plainer, and now, into the well-lighted road, a figure swung with long, wavering strides. It was not tall, but very spare, and was crowned with a bullet head set between high shoulders. But the face, as it flashed into and out of the narrow strip of moonlight, seemed strangely familiar, yet unnatural too.

Dan with difficulty repressed his exclamation of astonishment, and strained forward to make certain if this really were the man he took him to be. But turning neither to right nor left, the fellow plodded on, evidently in a labored way, and was almost instantly swallowed up in the shadows. The watcher drew a long breath.

"*Was* it Lozcoski?" he muttered presently. "Why, how did the man get out? And what does he want around here? He must be crazy to come into this neighborhood! If Murfree should know he wouldn't be comfortable, I reckon. I believe I ought to follow him and make certain somehow—I must! No telling what might happen, if they should meet."

He hurriedly led out his wheel, remounted it, and sped onward, determined to keep the man in sight. His amazement was great to find that the trail led straight as beaten paths would permit, to the very door of the new Social house, now filled with lights and people, and forming a conspicuous object in the little hamlet. Dan reached there but a rod or two behind his man, and saw him slip into the open doors and mingle with the crowd.

He began to think the likeness which had led him this last chase was an illusion, after all, and that the fellow must be some new workman, who had by chance discovered his woodland retreat and considered it public property.

But if that man were Lozcoski then Murfree ought to know. For, though Dan did not fancy the ranter and his ways, he was his close neighbor and belonged to the same union, which was reason enough why he owed him this duty.

Smoothing himself into shape as well as he could, the lad hid his wheel under the portico and stepped inside, trying to look bold in order to cover his bashful qualms, for he was as afraid of a social crowd as a fox of a pack of hounds. It was thoroughly brave of him to face these lights and people to warn a man not a special friend, and proved the loyal strain in his nature. Possibly, had he stopped to think, he might have weakened and fled. But the excitement of the chase still dominated him, and he had given himself no time for consideration before plunging in. Now, the buzz of talk and laughter sounded all about him; somebody slapped him on the back with a laugh of astonishment, and he began to realize what an impossible sort of thing he had done.

He wanted to turn and run out into the blessed darkness, but they hemmed him in, and, dazed by what seemed to him the luxury on every side, he hesitated and was lost. For, just

Fannie E. Newberry

then, a group of the younger people surged by and wrapped him around in a whirl of merry chaff.

"Hello! Here's Dan."

"Come along, Dan! Thought you wasn't going to any party, eh?"

"Couldn't stand it outside, could you, boy?"

"Thought to-morrow was your night, Dan, but you're welcome, old fellow!"

They seized him by each arm, and, overcoming his mute resistance, dragged him into the first parlor. He managed to wriggle loose after a bit, however, and watched his opportunity made a dart for the smaller one off, and rushed into an alcove somewhat in shadow, intending to escape entirely later on. As he stumbled into its shelter some one, half hidden by the tall back of a chair, turned and met him face to face. It was Rachel Hemphill, and she was as pale as he when she realized who had so summarily invaded her retreat.

"Why, Dan!" she said under her breath. "Is—are you—what has happened?"

"Sh-h! Rachel." He stepped past her and wedged himself in behind the chair, where he was well protected. "I've got no business here. I ain't dressed up. But I followed a man—I thought I knew him. Say, Rachel, do you remember Lozcoski?"

"Lozcoski? Why—oh, do you mean that low fellow that tried to fire the Works?"

"That's the fellow."

"Of course I do! Why?" She stepped closer and stood over him—she was taller than he—in such a way that no one could see him from the room beyond. "But Dan, he's in prison, isn't he? Don't you know how they said he raved and took on in his jargon, and nobody could understand him. He couldn't speak English at all, could he?"

"Not much. They managed to make out he was furious with Murfree, though—I suppose because he denounced him—and evidently was making threats against the old man. At any rate he kept up some kind of a howl about him all the time. I s'pose I ought to make sure, and let Murfree know, if 'tis him."

"You don't mean that Lozcoski's here, do you?"

"Well, that's the question. I—I wish you'd look him up for me, Rachel. I ain't fixed up for this, and I want to get out."

He spoke almost pathetically, shrinking back into his corner like a scared child, and Rachel's eyes began to dance. Something in the situation pleased her wonderfully. That Dan, who had scarcely spoken to her since the tragedy of his brother's death, should be cringing and pleading before her, all his prideful gloom quivering into a girlish terror of being seen in old clothes, was very satisfying to her. She would have liked to prolong the situation, but could not bring herself to torture her old playmate.

"I'll go, Dan," she whispered, "and you stay here till I get back. I'll bring Murfree to you, for he might not pay any attention to me. Nobody'll notice you if you keep this big chair before you. Just squat down on that round footstool thing in the corner. I'll be back in a minute."

Dan squatted, nodding meekly. Rachel adjusted the chair with attention, then hurried away, after a last glance at her captive, a new light on her really high-bred face. As she passed out into the hall she saw her mother in loud and busy talk, and hurried to her side.

"I've decided not to go quite yet," she said quickly, "so don't wait if you're ready."

"Oh, you have? What's up? Thought you was 'most tired to death just now. You don't look much tuckered, seems to me."

Rachel laughed lightly.

"Well, I'm beginning to find some fun in it, mother! I want to stay a little longer. I've got the shawl you sent me for—it lay on a big chair where you left it—and now I'm hunting up something else. Good-night, and don't wait for me."

She flitted on, her mother and companion gazing after her.

"Looks loike Rache has found a beau, or is looking for one," giggled Mother Flaherty, showing her yellow fangs with unpleasant recklessness. (This, you will remember, was before her accident.) But Mrs. Hemphill resented this with dignity.

"I guess you must 'a' forgot she and Will Price was keepin' comp'ny when that gun went off and shot him. She don't never say much—Rache don't—but she's gret to remember. And she ain't lookin' for beaux yet, I can tell you."

But the old Irishwoman only bobbed her wide cap borders to and fro and giggled again, as if not wholly convinced.

It was while Rachel thus stopped in the hall to speak with her mother that Larry was haranguing the crowd at the doors of the refreshment rooms, and when she presently returned to poor Dan, still crouched upon the hassock, her report was as follows:

"I saw Tonguey Murfree going in to supper with that handsome Miss Lavillotte—and a queer thing, too, for her to notice him, I thought—but all of a sudden he left her at the very door and rushed out through the front hall, so I guess he went home. But Dan, I had just a glimpse of a man pushing his way in, and it made me think of Lozcoski. But such a looking face! It was a mere glimpse, but I could only think of some animal. It wasn't just human. Do you suppose it was him?"

"Don't know," said Dan. "Anyhow it's all right, if Murfree keeps out of his way, and he will probably, if he's gone home. I'll stay till they come out from supper, and see the man again."

He said this in an odd voice, and did not look at Rachel. He seemed to be making concessions to somebody, and to be ashamed of doing it. After a look into his upraised eyes, which were full of a trouble she could not quite fathom, she dropped into the sheltering chair, and said gently,

"Dan, I've wanted a talk with you so long! Have I done anything to make you give me the cold shoulder? Or—or is it just that I make you think—of him?"

He threw up one hand, as if to ward off a blow.

"I can't let anybody talk about that. Don't Rachel!"

"I won't, I won't, Dan! I didn't mean to hurt you," soothingly. "But you make me feel, somehow, as if I had been doing

Fannie E. Newberry

something wrong to you, and you know I wouldn't, Dan. We were all such good friends together—then."

Her dark eyes looked down upon him pleadingly, and her fine face showed an emotion greater than her limited vocabulary could express in words.

Sometimes, though, words are less explanatory than looks. If Dan had once glanced up—but his eyes seemed glued to the floor. It was of hard wood, and its polished surface danced before him as he tried to steady himself to answer.

"I ain't blaming you," he muttered, "only—"

"Only what, Dan?"

He made a movement of his head that suggested a trapped animal, then suddenly stood up and looked at her, as if in desperation. She rose also, pale and startled.

"Don't you s'pose I know how you feel?" he murmured, while his large eyes glowed like coals in the shadows. "You're kind, but—but I don't want—pity. I know how I must seem to you, even if you try not to give up to it. When 'twas as it was I've got sense enough not to stay around and remind you—"

But just then there was a shout, a rush, excited cries and screams. Some one knocked over the chair which had screened them so loyally, and from which Rachel had just risen. Dan had caught one word, "Fight! Fight!" and conscience-smitten over his negligence in warning Murfree, sprang towards the hall from which the cries came, leaving Rachel alone. But she felt no special interest in a rough encounter between two men towards whom she was utterly indifferent. Their fate could not thrill her as did the memory of Dan's burning words. What did they mean? Had she the clue to conduct on his part which had grieved her sorely. She could not help a glow of expectation, and a thrill of pleasure. It was at this moment Joyce caught the radiant look on her face, and shared to a degree in that hidden gladness, through the sweet sympathy and friendliness of the glance she gave the girl who had half repulsed her but an hour, or two, before.

Fannie E. Newberry

CHAPTER XVII

DODO

It was a glorious morning. Joyce, romping around the lawn chased by Dodo, and much wound up with the cocker spaniel, Robin, did not see George Dalton as he entered her grounds from the front entrance, opposite the park. There was no reason why he should not mount the front steps and ring the doorbell, but a carriage-way led to a side entrance, and he felt certain that the gay laughter he could hear belonged to the person he had come to seek. So, guided by his ears, he followed this driveway till he could see the frolicking trio, then stopped abruptly before being himself discovered, and stepped behind a bed of tall cannas, where he deliberately peeped through the interstices of the massive foliage, his eyes shining with pleasure over the pretty sight.

It seemed a pity to him that he must tell his business and see that laughing young face settle into the maturer lines of thought and calculation. He would have liked to keep care and trouble far from it. But Robin, darting and tumbling about after a ball, pitched erratically in any direction but the right one from Dodo's plump little paw, soon found him out, and the puppy set up such a terrific barking as compelled attention.

"I surrender!" he cried, with a deprecating look at Joyce as he emerged. "I was just—just botanizing, you know." Delighted that she broke into merry laughter over the palpable fib he joined in, adding presently, "Pardon me, but you all looked so jolly! And you know I don't often see you this way."

"I should hope not!" hastily pinning up a stray tress, and wrapping her gown frills around a rent made by the over-eager spaniel. "Down, Robin, down! You tear one to pieces when you get so excited. Pray come in, Mr. Dalton, and Dodo dear, run home with Wobin a little while now. We'll finish our play later."

Before Dodo had time to raise a protest, Mr. Dalton broke in, pleadingly,

"Mightn't we sit here, Miss Lavillotte? I see chairs under the big tree, and it's so charming out there."

"Oh, yes," added Dodo, seeing her advantage, "we can tay out heah, Doyce, an' I'll talk to my doggy while you talk to—dat ozzer one," nodding her head shyly towards Dalton.

"Why Dodo!" cried the young hostess, half shocked, though wholly amused. But as Dalton again broke out she joined him, Dodo quite impersonally adding her cadenza.

She was delighted to feel that Joyce was not going to be sober and disagreeable with this visitor, and send her home before her play was out.

"I think we'll get on thus paired off—I and the other dog," he said, taking the chair Joyce indicated and dropping luxuriously back into its spreading seat, with his hands laid along its broad arms. "How delightful this is! Who could have dreamed, a twelve-month ago, that this scraggy bluff could be made into such beautiful homes, and that the dismal flat-iron below, dumping-place for tincans, frit, and cinders, as it was, could bloom out into that neat grassy park with growing trees along its walks, and flower-beds everywhere. Truly, money talks."

"Not money alone, Mr. Dalton. Something else must talk with it, seems to me."

"Oh, energy and taste to be sure."

"And good will."

"Granted, but—"

"Oh! Oh! Oh!" in shrieks from Dodo, who flies to Joyce's arms, Robin tearing beside her, vindictively shaking something limp and tousled in his sharp white teeth. "It's mine dolly, mine dolly. Oh, Doyce!"

The rag doll rescued from oblivion and Robin boxed, Mr. Dalton thought it time to introduce his business, and began:

"I came, as always, on a matter which concerns your affairs, Miss Lavillotte. I wanted to say—"

"Isn't my Doyce doin' to hab 'fweshments foh her comp'nay," broke in an insinuating little voice, in sweetest accents. "I comed back to tell you 'twould be perlite. Dat's de way my mamma does," and Dodo, first on one foot, then the other, performed a sort of fetish dance around the two, praying for the burnt offerings.

"Yes, yes, presently Dodo. Go on in, and ask Katie to send out cakes and lemonade, if you like. Now, Mr. Dalton."

"Yes, as I was about to say, I wanted—"

"Tan we hab tookies?" from Dodo.

"Of course, cookies if you want. Now run along!"

"Tan we hab toast-tookies?" persisted the bit of femininity.

Dodo had a way of lumping everything in the line of cookery that was brown and crisp under the name of "toast," from potatoes to pie. The cookies she referred to were simply a toothsome molasses cake, spread out thin and cut into crisp delicious squares, which Katie kept in a jar with rounded sides, after breaking apart. That jar was a mine of riches to the child, and those sweeties her pet confection. In fact, she had readily taken the large contract of keeping the jar from overflowing, and was the principal consumer of "toast cookies." Smiling helplessly, Joyce assented.

"Yes, toast-cookies it shall be."

She gave the child a little push and nodded towards her manager to urge haste. He galloped ahead.

"I wanted to say that this escaped criminal does prove to be Lozcoski, the man I told you of who attempted once to fire the Works. He had heaped kindlings, dipped in kerosene, wherever a bit of woodwork gave opportunity to start a blaze. He was caught by Murfree, and—"

"I telled her, Doyce," panting with the haste of her precipitate return. "I telled her, and she said 'Umph!' but I dess she will. Say, Doyce—"

"Hush, Dodo! Mr. Dalton is talking, and you *must* be quiet. Shall I hold you?"

Fannie E. Newberry

"No, no, I don't want to be church-'till. I want to womp."

"Well, go and 'womp' then, bless you! And be quick about it."

"But I wants to eat first."

"Talk fast, Mr. Dalton. She is pouting now, and you may get in a sentence or two."

He met her merry look with a very kindly one.

"I see you *can* be patient, Miss Lavillotte. Well, as this Lozcoski set fire to your Works and was imprisoned on that indictment, he has been rearrested to serve out his sentence. He escaped from prison one night when a fire in the dormitories had demoralized the discipline. He—"

"It's tomin'! It's tomin'! Dere's de lemmade and tookies, Doyce. See, see?"

The young lady put a white hand over the child's restless lips and nodded vigorously towards her manager, who continued rapidly:

"He hid in the woods till that night of the party, waiting for a chance at Murfree, I presume, for he is bitter against him yet. But, driven desperate by hunger, he came into town, and the smell and sight of the feasting nearly crazed him, I imagine. So—"

"Doyce! Doyce! Heah's Katie waitin'. Where'll we hab de table? Why don't you pay 'tention to Katie? Where's de table-cloff? Oh, oh, if she puts it down on dat twee-bench Wobin will eat it all up!"

Joyce put out a warning hand again, and kept her eyes

on Dalton's.

"And so—and so—dear me! I'm all in a mix-up. Can't remember what I was going to say, but the gist is, you will have to go into court to swear something—"

"Doyce, I fink you is aw-wful naughty! Pooh Katie is *so* tired."

"Well, you see Mr. Dalton—it's no use. Let us eat and drink, for to-morrow we die! Dodo, you are the great American nuisance, in person. Katie, give me that tray and run back for the little rustic stand in the arbor—oh, thank you, Mr. Dalton! Now, Dodo, sit down there and don't speak till you have eaten that cookie all up."

"Two tookies, Doyce. Two-o tookies!"

"Very well, two or twenty, only that you remain tongue-tied meanwhile. Shall I give you a glass, Mr. Dalton?"

"It's dood!" from Dodo, sipping ecstatically from her special little mug, filled by Katie, and taking great scalloping bites out of her square cake, while Robin, planted directly before her, but as quiveringly as if on coiled springs, watched every bite, snapping his own jaws each time in acutest sympathy.

"Yes, and two-o tookies, please," laughed the man with a warm feeling of comfort and sweetness wrapping him round like a soft blanket. "And let's give it up for a while and be happy."

"Why not?" returned Joyce, obliviously. "Here's the plate of cakes at your elbow. Eat them all if you will. There are plenty more."

A shriek from Dodo, who has dropped half of hers and seen it incontinently snapped up and gorged by Robin. Of course the shriek ends in a choking cough, as her mouth is full, and Mr. Dalton has to snatch her up and turn her face downwards, while Joyce paddles her little back till the morsel is ejected. When they have all got their breaths again—the dog meanwhile having sneaked a whole cake from the plate and fled to a safe distance—they subside into a restful silence for a space. George Dalton's hair is somewhat rumpled, and Joyce's cheeks are red. Neither laughs outright, but both long to. It is a decided relief from the tension when a maid appears from the other house, and Miss Dodo is carried off for her nooning nap, kicking vigorously. They sit back and sip their iced drinks relishingly. The morning is warm and Joyce's lovelocks are tightly curled against her wet forehead. She mops it daintily with a bit of cambric and lace, and he watches her silently, while the branches of the tree above his head sway softly against each other, and the leaves whisper confidingly way up in the clear ether.

The busy man feels the charm of it as he has seldom felt such things before, and Joyce feels his pleasure and is glad over it, but secretly thinks it quite time for him to finish his business and be gone. Her appearance is far from tidy, and she is half expecting a friend from the city out to luncheon. At length, in a dreamy way, he takes up the narrative so often interrupted.

"I was going to give a few more details about the Pole. You knew about the way he acted in the Social-house—his ravenous ways over the food?"

"Yes, I saw him," shuddering a little.

"He had been starving for three days. The officers were fast on his track and arrested him hot from the fight. Had he not seen Murfree I presume he would have made his way back to the woods safely. But they came in by train just in time to learn of his queer actions and nab him. Not a minute too soon, either. He had nearly choked the life out of his accuser."

"How is Murfree, Mr. Dalton?"

"Pretty well used up. I never saw him so completely cowed. It knocked all the eloquence out of him for once. The man is a crank and an agitator. I have kept my eye on him for some time. He is a fairly good workman in his line, though, and just now can't do much harm, as times are easy and these new improvements of yours keep the people busy with other interests. But he would stir them all up, if he could."

"And the other—Lozcoski—is he in prison again?"

"No, he was hurt, too. He is in the jail hospital. What with his starving and all, he is quite ill. There is some legal hitch, too, about his re-commitment, and you and I are to be summoned to testify as to various matters concerning the Works. It will necessitate a journey into town. And shall I plan to go with you?" He was quite the business manager again.

"Certainly, if you will be so kind."

"I would advise taking Mr. Barrington with us to the jail. He can coach us as to details."

"Yes," said Joyce thoughtfully. "And we must try and get at the bottom of the affair this time. Must you go now?" for he had risen with a resolute air.

"Indeed I must. I don't know when I have spent such a

lazy—and happy—morning!"

"Next time we'll have to banish naughty Dodo. Isn't she a persistent baby?"

"A very charming one, though. Good-morning!"

He made her a stiff little bow, and hurried away without so much as one look behind him. But as he passed the next house, and heard a voice near some upper window crooning a lullaby, he smiled to himself, and whispered,

"Blessed little Dodo! Sweet sleep and happy dreams."

CHAPTER XVIII

NATE TIERNEY

The heated spell was succeeded by a week of chilling rains. These made the children appreciate the arcade leading from the park to the school-house, and one afternoon they were romping up and down its cement roadway, just after school was out. Even Mrs. Hemphill's younger brood was there, for the delight of the youngsters in their classes, which embraced lessons in carpentry, husbandry, electrical science, cookery, sewing, nursing, and so on, had so infected them that they simply could not be kept at home.

Joyce's school, planned to the least detail, under the Madame's instruction, was not quite like any other known. Text-books were used, to be sure, and classes were, in a sort, graded, but books played a smaller part than usual in the teachings of each day, and every task of the pupils was so put into actual practice as to make it a lesson of experience, if possible.

For instance, little Tirza Hemphill, before she learned to rattle off her table of dry measure, as other school children do, had discovered its scale for herself, by practical application. A series of measures was set out in a row, from pint to bushel, while a great box of shelled corn stood by,

Fannie E. Newberry

and she was told to begin with the smallest in order to find out for herself how many times it must be emptied into the next to fill it, and so on to the bushel. The increased size of the receptacle here, made it necessary to take the rest on trust, but being assured by actual measurement that the pints, quarts, and bushels were correct, she was prepared to believe the rest.

As to the classes in needle-work, cookery, and house service, they answered the purpose of recesses between the book lessons, and were considered great fun by the girls, while the boys equally enjoyed their hammering, out-door husbandry, and telegraph operating.

It took room, but they had plenty of that in Littleton, and one part of the ample school grounds was the farm and garden. It took tools, and they cost money, but some were very primitive, often made by the more ingenious lads, them-selves; and when Wolly of the unpronounceable surname actually made a little wheeled cultivator, the harrow being the tooth from a broken horse-rake, and the two wheels a relic from a defunct doll-wagon, he was considered the hero of the school. It took a stove and kitchen, but they used the one in the Social-house, going to and fro in procession, with a teacher in charge.

It was indeed a novel school, and one just out from a stiff, starched, eastern graded Grammar school might have raised his hands in holy horror. Still there was no lack of method, nor of discipline, and each class, be it held out-doors or in, was made to understand that good work was required. All was orderly enough, even when the noon class went through the ceremony of serving a neat meal, and eating it in quiet decency.

The older pupils were intensely interested in the banking

class, the teacher acting as president, and two or three being chosen as cashier, teller, and clerk. They were furnished with neatly stamped coins and bills, such as are sold for toy money, and the rest of the class became depositors and learned how to draw and deposit, to count readily, to make change, to make out checks, to compute interest, discount bills, buy drafts, etc., etc.

Once Mr. Dalton asked Joyce, with that cynicism which belonged to him,

"Why do you have the poor little beggars taught this sort of business? That they may learn to value the money they may never possess?" and she had flashed around upon him with the answer,

"They will possess it! Do you for an instant believe our scholars are to be kept in bondage to one solitary trade? They will not all be glass-blowers, I can promise you."

In fact, already these little financiers were substituting real money for the spurious pretense, and Saturday mornings they came to deposit their penny savings in the bank kept by their teacher, or to draw, with interest, their savings of weeks. In order to encourage frugality, this interest was compounded, after the principal had been left in bank for three months, silver to be returned where only copper had been deposited. Behind all this stood Joyce's useful millions and the Madame's guiding hand.

It was not a great while before the mothers began to come in with their petty savings, also, and after a long talk with Mr. Barrington, one day, a real banking institution was incorporated, with the stock issued in dollar shares. Mr. Barrington, as president, headed the list of stockholders with a hundred, Miss Lavillotte following with seventy-five, while Mr. Dalton, Madame Bonnivel, and Larry Driscoll were all down for fifty, or less.

It was a delightful little bank, where pennies stood for dollars, where everyone had confidence in everybody else, where no other banks could make or break, and where the assets were so in excess of the liabilities that it could not be touched by panic. Every three months there was to be a change of clerks, though the officers were retained. This was to give each scholar an opportunity of learning all the practical routine of a bank, also, to offer facilities for the handling and counting of money.

I have enlarged upon the bank more than its relative importance warrants. Really, the domestic economy classes were given greater prominence in the school, and the changes these well-taught children gradually introduced into their sordid home life were many and excellent.

Mother Flaherty was so electrified over the tin of light, sweet rolls her little grand-daughter made for supper, one evening, that she caught it up with the dish-towel and ran a block to Mrs. Hemphill's, to display the golden-brown beauties before allowing one of the family to touch them. But, a few days later, Mrs. Hemphill, not to be outdone, invited Mother Flaherty in to tea, and they were served to a neat little meal by Tirza and Polly, where every article, from the smoking-hot croquettes to the really delicate custard and cakes, was the work of these two little girls. It was an honest rivalry, which hurt nobody, and the men, better fed at their evening meal, began to linger at home to join in the children's geographical and other games, picked up at school, or to accompany their families over to the Social-house, to listen to the orchestra made up of their older sons, to hear Miss Lavillotte play and sing, to witness an exhibition of kinetoscope pictures, or sometimes just to meet other friends and simply bask in the light and ease of the pretty rooms. They almost forgot Lon's place, even, as they gazed contentedly about, and enjoyed the bright open fire in the immense hall grate, which these cool nights made welcome.

While the pendulum of our narrative has been swinging back and forth through these many months of effort, the children whom we left playing in the arcade are still awaiting us, enjoying their out-door freedom, but well protected by its roof from the damp weather. Their modes of playing are not quite the same as those of a year ago. There is boisterousness, to be sure, but less cruelty, and far less profanity. The dogs join merrily in the frolics, now, with no dread of old tin-can attachments, and even little crippled Dosey Groesbeck lingers about on his crutches, not expecting them to be knocked from under him, as used to be the case.

They are cleaner, also, for it is not true that the poor naturally love dirt. They get used to it, because often they have no conveniences for bathing, and sometimes every drop of water must be sought at a distant hydrant, and carried up two or three rickety flights of stairs before available for use. This makes it so precious that they learn to do without it. Joyce never forgot the picture of one little waif of two years, brought in from the streets, taking its first warm bath in a tub, an embodiment of delight, splashing, laughing, dipping, screaming, in a very ecstasy of happiness. Repeatedly, the attendant tried to remove her, only to yield to her cries and entreaties against her own judgment, until the little creature had to be forcibly removed and consoled with a new wonder—a delicious cup of warm, creamy milk in which sweet cracker had been crumbled. Accepting her change of heavens with tranquillity, the new Ariadne fell asleep in the warm enveloping blanket, worn out with sheer pleasure.

So the Littleton children, having the bathing facilities of the rich, if not on so gorgeous a scale, were a really trim, decent lot to-day, and their merry voices reached Nate Tierney, going rapidly along the street, outside, making him waver, hesitate, then turn in, with a smile on his honest face. He was a favorite with the younglings. With cries of "Nate! Nate!" "Hello, Nate!" "Be on my side, Nate!" they surrounded him, and dragged him into their game of Indian-and-white man, a willing captive.

"Well now," he laughed, "do you think it's quite fair to turn a feller into an injun off hand, like that? However, if I've got to be one, I'll be an awful one, you bet: A red, ramping, roaring old Apache, that'll think nothing o' scalping and toma-hawking everything he can ketch. Be off now, or I'll snatch the whole pack of you, and make you run the gauntlet. One—two—three—GO."

They were off, shrieking with excited fun, all white men for the minute, with one big Indian driving them before him. The arcade could not contain them in this wild rush for safety, and they streamed into and across the park, Nate at their backs, giving the most approved Apache war-whoop between his shouts of laughter.

As he stopped in the street beyond, out of breath, calling merrily, between his gasps, that they weren't playing fair to run so far and leave him all alone, he noticed his friend, Hapgood, just turning in at the door of his now neat cottage, further down the block. He stopped yelling to give the man a critical stare.

"Off his base a bit, hey?" he muttered. "Stepped into Lon's as he come by, and didn't stop at one glass, nuther. If Bill warn't sech an all-round good feller I'd call him a fool! A man 'ts got jest a wife might look into a glass now and then. Like as not she could bring him to time, if he went too far. When he's got wife and children both, he oughter go it easy and stop off short and quick; but when he's got children and no wife, and just a slim little gal like Lucy to look after things, why, he ought never even to look toward a green door? I ain't no teetotaller, goodness knows! But men 't ain't got no sense oughtn't to be fathers. Guess that's why I'm an old bach," laughing a little.

The children, swarming back with taunting cries, broke in upon his meditations, and dragged him into one more race. He was bounding nimbly after them, the young pack in full cry, when he saw something that froze his blood, and stopped him as suddenly as if by a wall of rock. It was Lucy, wild-eyed and white-faced, dashing out of the house-door, while close at her heels raced her father, a stick of stove wood raised in air, as if to strike. Liquor and passion had made him an utter maniac for the minute. Clasped close in the poor girl's arms was the little baby, its head pressed so tightly against her breast that it could not cry out. Lucy, flying for life, was evidently too spent and breathless to make a sound, either.

With a hoarse cry of horror, Nate took a great leap forward and flung himself, with the fury of a mad bull, between the girl and her natural protector, meeting Hapgood's onslaught with head down and hands extended. The latter, blind with his insensate fury, plunged ahead, unable to stop himself if he would. It looked as if Nate's skull would be laid open with the billet of wood.

But just as Hapgood would have felled the obstruction, neither knowing nor caring what it might be, he stubbed his toe and went down like a log, the stick flying out of his hand, and hitting the ground harmlessly just beyond. In an instant Nate had grasped it, and stood over the prostrate inebriate in his turn. It is well said, "Beware the fury of a patient man."

Slow Nate Tierney was white to his lips, now, beneath the bronze of years, and the knotted veins of his temples throbbed perceptibly. For perhaps the first time in his life he was thoroughly angry.

"Lie there, you brute! You scum!" he cried in a deep harsh voice, unrecognizable as his own. "You'll chase your own children, will you? You'll hit your little Lucy with sticks like this, will you? And she savin' the poor baby in her arms. Dog! I've a mind to brain you where you lie."

The scared children, looking on, wondered if this could indeed be Nate. The drunken man on the ground, winking and blinking through bleared eyes, tried to remember if he had ever seen that marble-faced avenger before. Lucy, peering fearfully through the front window behind locked doors, hardly knew which to dread the more, her passionate unreasoning father, or this new and strange edition of her good-natured old friend.

Nobody spoke or moved for an instant, while Nate stood there, the man's life in his hand, then slowly he lowered the uplifted weapon, caught Hapgood by the collar, and dragged him to his feet.

"I won't soil my hands with the killing of you, Bill Hapgood!" he muttered. "The cage is the place for mad dogs, and there you go. Now march!"

"Now Nate, what you up to?" whined the other, pretty well sobered by all this. "Le' go o' me, can't you? 'Tain't any of your funerals, is it?"

"It may be if I kill you," was the grim answer. "March!" and he gave the wretched Hapgood a smart tap with his improvised billy that sent him on several paces.

Then, to his utter discomfiture, out popped Lucy, red with indignation.

"Nate Tierney, what you doing with my father? Where you going to take him to? Let him alone, I say. Let him alone!" Her voice rang out shrilly, as she came forward, trembling with anger, and her knight-errant looked up at her in a daze of wonderment. Could this be Lucy?

"I'm a-goin' to take him where he won't have a chance at you again very soon, child," he answered gently. "I'm a-goin' to put him in the lock-up."

"The lock-up!" shrieked Lucy.

"The lock-up?" yelled the children.

"The lock-up!" roared the prisoner, galvanized into action by this supreme horror. With one mighty effort he wrenched himself loose and turned upon Nate, fighting like a tiger.

It was a short battle. Taken by surprise Tierney was for a minute overpowered, but as he felt his only weapon, the stick, slipping from his grasp he put forth all his strength and caught it back with a desperate grip. Half fallen backward in the struggle he made a wild pass in the air. He heard a crashing noise that seemed to rend his own soul apart. Then the thud of a heavy body as it fell. And then, heaven and earth seemed to stand still for one awful minute as, feeling no further resistance, he raised himself and looked down upon his friend, William Hapgood. Inert and still he lay, with his skull crushed in just above the left temporal bone.

CHAPTER XIX

IN THE CAGE

Sometimes an eternity of suffering is condensed into a single minute, yet that suffering is so like a dream, because of the paralyzed brain, that one cannot fully realize it until afterwards. As Nate Tierney stood over his victim, nerveless and faint, with eyeballs starting from their sockets, he realized the lowest deep of hell, yet as if it had been another man whose agony he looked upon. It was quite beyond his own enduring. Lucy's horrified shriek brought him more fully to his senses, and the screams of the children who scattered in every direction, crying as they ran on, only to creep back after a moment drawn by that prurient curiosity which is the one natural tie left between the buzzard and man.

It afterward seemed to Nate as if in that one horrible, helpless minute a hundred shapes had suddenly encompassed him, risen out of the earth perhaps, so rapidly did they crowd about him, hemming him in. Amid the wild confusion some one thought to summon the marshal, another Mr. Dalton, still another the doctor, and these three strode upon the scene in time to see poor Nate lifting his old friend's head, to whisper hoarsely,

"Oh, Bill! I didn't mean it. I didn't mean it!" in a wail that would have melted granite.

He looked up as Dr. Browne thrust everybody aside, and begged pitifully:

"Oh, can't you mend it, doctor? It's broke in, but can't you mend it? I didn't go to do it. I just swung the stick. Can't you mend it?"

The doctor knew at the first glance that there was no mending for that mortal hurt. But it was hard to say so in answer to that wild white face quivering at his feet.

"Get back, Nate," he said kindly, stooping to the body. "I'll see what can be done. Let somebody that's stronger than her help to carry him," and at his gesture, two or three onlookers stepped forward obeying ward.

As they lifted the lifeless form, Nate, still stupidly kneeling beside it as if unable to move, the slow-dripping blood from that crushed temple fell on his upturned face, and trickled down into the stubble of his unshorn beard. Lucy, amid her frantic cries, saw it and fell back half fainting, into the arms of Babette, who hastily led her away inside her own rooms, assisted by Rachel, who came quickly to her aid. The baby, nearly dropping from her sister's nerveless arms, was caught by Dan before it reached the ground, and the little thing clung to him, wailing feebly in its fright and misery. So, not knowing what else to do, he followed the girls indoors, a part of the women pressing after. But most of the crowd trailed in the wake of the little procession which was being led by the doctor into the Hapgood cottage, only to be promptly shut out at the door.

Dalton went inside with the doctor, but the marshal put a hand on Nate's shoulder, and said under his breath,

Fannie E. Newberry

"Come, Tierney."

Nate looked at him dully.

"Yes, indeed, I'll do anything for him, anything you say. Won't they let me sit by him, don't you think?"

The man of law looked into the other's face amazedly. Didn't he understand yet? he wondered.

"You can't do anything now," he said. "Just come along wi' me. Don't you know what you've done, man alive?"

Nate looked at him an instant and staggered where he stood.

"Go on," he said thickly, after that one instant's horrified perception. "I'm ready," and he spoke no more.

The marshal hustled him quickly through the crowd and down the street, to the little building known as the lock-up. It was the place to which he had meant to consign Hapgood a bit ago. The crowd buzzing after like flies around a dead horse, surged up to the door and leaned against it, outside. It was a small square building, scarcely larger than a smokehouse, with two tiny barred windows up under its roof, and one thick door, clamped with iron, in front. It was built of stone laid in cement up to within three feet of the eaves, and finished out with timber. There was no way of heating it, and it held absolutely no movable furniture. A bunk projected two feet from one of the cemented walls, eighteen inches above the stone floor, bare planks, without mattress or blanket. That was all. A cage, indeed, as Nate had called it in his anger of a short time since, which had so completely vanished now. But he little cared for its bareness in that misery of the soul which so far transcends bodily suffering.

"I'll bring you in a blanket and a comfortable of my wife's to make up your bed, and a basin and pitcher of water. I don't want to be hard on an old chum. I'll fix you up real snug while you stay, and you just try and settle down to make the best of it. You can't gather up spilled milk, Nate, nor spilled blood, neither. Now I'm going, but I'll come back pretty soon, and don't worry."

Nate still did not answer, nor move. But as the door closed heavily his lips parted.

"Dead! Dead! No, *no*, NO!" and a strong shudder took possession of him, as uncontrollable as an ague fit.

When the marshal returned, a few moments later, with the comforts he had promised, Nate still sat there, gray, haggard, and speechless. The kind-hearted jailer looked askance at him, and hesitated to ask him to rise that he might arrange the bunk. When he did proffer the request Nate stared at him a moment, as if unhearing, then slowly rose and looked down at the planks he had been sitting on, seemingly seeing them for the first time. Then he continued the survey, letting his eyes, already bloodshot with excitement and misery, scan the narrow place.

"So," he said finally, in a low, hoarse whisper, smiling up into the officer's face with an expression that almost started the tears even to those hardened orbs, "So, you're going to bury us both—Bill and me. Him in a grave and me in a tomb—Bill and me. I never thought 'twould be like that— Bill and me. Buried together—Bill and me." He continued to mutter the words over and over, and when the keeper left the building he shook his head sadly.

"Poor Nate! It's touchin' him in the brain, I reckon. Hope he won't lose his reasons afore the trial comes on, though. He'll need 'em then if he ever does. Blarst his foolishness! What did he mix in for, anyhow?"

CHAPTER XX

SORROW

Joyce had just returned from a half day in the city with Camille, whom she had been treating to some first-class music, and was just crossing the lawns to her own door, when she saw George Dalton come swiftly across the road from the park. She turned towards the walk to greet him, but her happy face fell as she saw the perturbed expression upon his.

"What is it?" she asked, looking down upon him from the ascending walk, which led somewhat steeply up to her veranda steps. "There is some trouble?"

"Yes." He gained her vicinity with a long stride, and said gently, "It's trouble beyond even your helping, this time. Lucy Hapgood's father is dead."

"Dead? Why, has he been ill? I didn't know. Why wasn't I told sooner?"

"No, not ill. He was killed—struck down in anger by Nate Tierney."

"By Nate? Good Nate, who has been so kind; who was such

Fannie E. Newberry

a friend? I can't believe it!"

"Nor I, hardly. Only poor Bill is dead with a broken skull, and Nate in the lock-up. The man—Hapgood, of course—came home drunk, and began abusing Lucy. Nate saw her running from him and snatched the billet of wood that her father was chasing her with. Then they fought, and Bill was finished. It happened not two hours ago."

You will perceive that Dalton told the story as he had heard it, not just as it happened. But his version was the one generally accepted at that time. Joyce clasped her hands together with a passionate movement.

"Dreadful! Dreadful! Poor Lucy; poor Nate!"

"You don't say poor Bill, Miss Lavillotte."

"No, it is the living who are to be pitied here, and Nate most of all. He did it for Lucy's sake, I know; it was to save her from her father's fury. There can be no doubt of that. Did you say that he is already in the lock-up? Where is that?"

He told her.

"I must go to Lucy first," she mused. "How does the poor child bear it?"

"Badly for a time, but she is more quiet now. The French sisters and Rachel are with her, and a lot of other women, who might be spared."

"Miss Joyce, dinner is ready," called Ellen from the veranda with a sour voice, for she resented being kept waiting.

"Come in and eat with us," said Joyce, laying a hand lightly on Dalton's arm. "It will not take us long, and then I can go with you. Won't you, please?"

He colored with pleasure, for her manner was most friendly. Just so might she speak to Mr. Driscoll, he thought.

The little meal was something of a revelation to the man. Ellen carved, and a neat maid handed the plates about on a silver salver. There were flowers on the table, and little else, it seemed to him. Yet, as one course followed another, he felt it to be a bountiful meal, even for the healthy man's appetite that he possessed. It did not please his palate any better than his aunt's excellent dinners, but he felt there were intricacies and embellishments in some of these unknown dishes that her best skill had never compassed. He began with some nervousness, but Joyce's simple, homelike manner soon dispelled it, and they ended over the fruit and coffee in most friendly converse, he telling, she hearing, many particulars of the Hapgood family, that were new to her.

Long before he had concluded Joyce was smiling over a thought which had been growing upon her for some time. George Dalton was not so indifferent to these people of hers as he would often try to appear. Evidently he watched them, understood them, even, possibly, sympathized with them. They were not mere machines to him, as she had once felt they were. He did have an interest that was close and personal, and not wholly of a business character, however much he might try to conceal it under his cool manner.

They soon reached the Hapgood door, around which still clustered a crowd of the neighbors, the men stolidly smoking, the women whispering in detached groups, all with that expectant air which attends upon a tragic incident. They made way respectfully for the manager, but looked somewhat wonderingly upon his companion, probably questioning what could be her interest in the event. Dalton pushed through the press, keeping her close in his wake. But once within the door no conventional barriers were interposed. The gloomy distance and silence attendant upon the last hours of the great were not in the way of friendly sympathy, or unfriendly intrusion, here. The back door stood wide open, and people came and went, while the children's sobs mingled with the curt, outspoken directions of the undertaker and the clatter of dishes, which some obliging neighbor was washing at the kitchen sink. The body of the murdered man lay on the bed in a small room off the little sitting-room—an apartment so tiny that the door had to be left open, so that the implements of this last service to his body might overflow into the larger room. Lucy, pale and swollen-eyed, was rocking the baby before the little gas grate, with her back that way, the child with wide, wakeful eyes gazing solemnly up into her suffering face, trying vainly to puzzle out the situation. Babette, a pretty girl with a rose and lily face, was soothing Rufie and Tilly near by, while Mrs. Hemphill, with her own baby in her arms, kept a sharp lookout both on this little group, and upon the two men in the small bedroom. It seemed to Joyce that the place was aswarm with bustling humanity, and struck her with a sharp pang that the little children should see and hear so much of these gruesome details. Just as they entered Mrs. Hemphill's high-pitched voice was making a remark—

"No, 'tain't easy to dispose of young'uns that's left orphans. Children's like tooth-picks—most folks prefers their own," and Joyce could imagine why Lucy's expression was so tense and drawn.

She stepped quickly to the young girl's side and, stooping, tenderly kissed her cheek. Lucy looked up wonderingly an instant, then burst into a fresh flood of tears, while Joyce held the weary little head against her side, smoothing its pretty hair with soft fingers, but saying no word. Presently the bereaved girl sobbed out, "It's so good of you to come!" and she answered softly, "I was glad to, Lucy. I want you to let me help in someway." She drew a chair forward and looked at the unwinking baby, but did not offer to take it. She felt that the sister drew quietness and comfort from the warmth and pressure of its little body. But in gentle tones she began asking questions of Babette as to the plans and needs for the next few days; and, in listening to her suggestions and promises of assistance, Rufie and Tilly ceased sobbing and drew closer, while even Lucy soon leaned forward, talking unreservedly. The baby, seeing that normal conditions were apparently restored, at last began to blink, and finally fell away into happy dreamland. When Joyce rose to go a sense of comfort pervaded the group. Lucy, fully assured that her father would be laid away with fitting ceremony and that she and the children—though what was she but a child herself, poor thing!—should be decently arrayed in mourning apparel, began to take on a less worried expression. As she also rose, to lay the baby aside on an old lounge in the corner, where the older baby was already asleep, Joyce beckoned to Dalton and conferred with him a minute, then drew on her wrap, to leave.

As Lucy turned, the manager spoke a few words to her.

"Oh, will you, sir?" cried the girl as he finished. "My! but that takes a load offen me. And I can stay in the dear little house, and keep the children, just like I allays did!"

He nodded, and Lucy glanced with a perplexed look from him to Joyce.

"Seems like you're both doing this, and I ought to thank you both," she said. "I was feeling pretty bad before you come in. I couldn't see nothing ahead but to put the children in a

Fannie E. Newberry

Home and go out to service, and—and it 'most killed me!" her lips quivering anew.

Joyce smiled and took her hand.

"Thank him," she said, with a glance up into his eyes. "But you can keep a few kind thoughts for me too, Lucy. I will take it upon myself to attend to your mourning, as I said."

"And you won't forget the veil, Miss Lavillotte?"

"No indeed!" smiling down into the eager young face. "But Lucy"—she bent closer, to speak just above a whisper—"I'm going to poor Nate, now. Have you no kind message to send to him?"

"No, *no!*" came out sharply, like a suppressed shriek. "He did it! How could I?"

"But to help you, child. It is terrible, I know, and I will not press the matter if it is more than you can bear to speak of it. But, surely, you feel that what Nate did was not intentional? He was shielding you, defending you. Oh, Lucy I would not arraign your father, but I can't help pitying poor Nate, who has been such a friend to you!"

Lucy turned abruptly and went towards the fire, where she stood a moment, shivering perceptibly, a desolate little figure. Soon she raised her head, flung a glance towards Mrs. Hemphill, whose watchful eyes were gloating over the scene, then with a beckoning look towards Joyce walked to the back door. Joyce instantly followed her, leaving her escort in low-toned talk with the undertaker.

"I can't say a word before her," whispered Lucy with a backward jerk of her thumb, "she tattles so! Nate used to tell me not to. But about—I—I can't send no word. He killed my father? Don't you see? *He killed my father.*"

There was such an intensity of trouble and despair in the whisper that it started tears in the eyes of Joyce.

"I can only repeat, my dear, it was not intentional. He was beside himself with trouble and passion; and it was all for you."

"Yes, but 'twas awful, awful! Pa was the red-mad kind, you see; so hot and spunky you couldn't do nothing but run from it. You knew it didn't mean much—just a tantrum that he'd come out of slick enough byme-by, and then be good as pie to make up. But Nate's! 'Twas the awful white-mad kind. I never saw it in him before, and I could see it meant a whole lot. It scared all my scare about pa right out of me. It—I can't tell you how it made me feel! 'Twas like seeing into the bad place, I guess. I knew something had got to break, and it did. 'Twas poor pa's skull. How can I dare to say good words to Nate, when *he* lies like that in there?"

She pointed backward with a gesture that was tragic in its simplicity, and Joyce could scarcely find words for further argument. But her keen sympathy was with Nate. She had that rare tenderness which goes with acute perceptions, and cannot be complete without them. She could put herself in another's place and actually feel another's woes. She felt poor Tierney's so strongly that she sent up a prayer for guidance before answering, very softly, "My child, Christ forgave from the very cross."

"But you see I can't *forgive*, because—Oh, you don't know, you don't know. I'm so awful, so wicked!"

She pressed her clasped hands before her mouth as if to shut

Fannie E. Newberry

something back, while Joyce gazed at her, perplexed and uncomprehending.

"You can't forgive, Lucy? Perhaps not, just yet. But you can pity. Let me at least tell poor Nate that you are sure he would not have done it only in great anger, and you'll try to forgive him. Mayn't I say that?"

"Y-yes, make it up any way you like only—only—"

"Only what, Lucy?"

But the girl shook her head.

"I can't tell you. You don't understand. Just say anything you want to."

She turned and ran indoors, then popped out again and sprang down the steps.

"Miss Lav'lotte."

"Yes."

"Please don't forget the black hat and veil. Have it very heavy, and very black, and very long, won't you? Oh pa, poor, poor pa!" and, breaking into loud wailing, Lucy disappeared within.

The girl's manner puzzled Joyce. It seemed to her that Lucy attached immense importance to so trivial a thing as a mourning veil, yet she could not feel that this was all girlish frivolity and shallowness. Something in the child's whole manner disputed such a suggestion. Neither was her attitude towards Nate quite clear. She said she could not forgive, yet instinctively Joyce felt that neither did she entirely condemn.

Could it be that deep within her she not only forgave, but condoned, and that her almost feverish desire to appear in the trappings of extreme woe was induced by the consciousness that she was not so filled with resentment and horrified grief as she ought to be?

She was still revolving these queries when Dalton joined her and led her around to the front, debouching so as to avoid the few scattered groups still outside. He did not offer his arm, but kept close at her side, ready to aid instantly should she make a misstep amid the unfamiliar surroundings. Once he steadied her as she slipped from the single plank that made the walk around the cottage, but instantly withdrew his sustaining hand. Not until they were walking along the street, with its electric lights at each intersection, did either speak. Then Joyce asked suddenly,

"Will Lucy ever consent to see Nate again? Can the old-time friendship help, in any degree, to soften her towards him?" George looked down upon the sweet face beside him, so filled with sympathy and concern, and checked some impulse to answer hastily. After a little he said in a deliberate voice, as if weighing each word,

"Dear Miss Lavillotte, when death comes into a life like yours it means grief, pure and simple. Other thoughts and interests are put aside. There is no compulsion, no haste. They can wait. But it is not so with the people we have been to see. There is so much besides the simple sense of loss and bereavement. A thousand anxieties crowd so closely the holier sorrow is half shut out. Sometimes, much as we shrink from acknowledging it, the gain is more than the loss. Perhaps it leaves fewer mouths to feed. Perhaps it takes away a continual menace and terror. You can't conceive of feeling that a father means only a—tormentor. But—think of it."

He felt Joyce shiver beside him, and stopped abruptly, shaken by a sudden consciousness that had never before occurred to him. Could it be that out of her own experience she did comprehend? She looked up piteously and her face was white in the dusk.

"Yes, I could," she murmured in a husky whisper. "I know, I understand."

He dared not speak he was so filled with emotion. It had rushed over him in a flood. To think she had suffered so— *she*! In a minute her plaintive voice broke upon him once more.

"It's like this. Lucy can't be so sorry as she ought to be, and it is dreadful to her. It is like those fearful dreams when we long to get somewhere and cannot take a step, or ache to cry out and cannot make a sound. She aches to feel sorrier; she is ashamed that she cannot. But grief sits back and laughs at hers, and will not be coaxed into her company. It nearly kills her that it is so, for she is a good, conscientious girl who wants to do and to be right—oh, poor little Lucy!"

He took her shaking hand and drew it gently within his arm. She was weeping behind her veil, and he felt the passion in her outburst. He was not stupid; he had known James Early. He could feel to his soul what was passing in hers, and the revelation wrung him as no sorrow had ever wrung him before. If he but dared to comfort her, to assure her that here was a friend who would stand between her and every wrong in future! After a little he dared trust himself to answer.

"Miss Lavillotte, I think life is always harder than it looks from the outside—yet easier, too. At the worst something comes to help out. And, just because it is so hard, it can be no sin to be glad and happy when Heaven gives us the chance. No decent person will kick a man when he is down; neither does fate. When you talk to Lucy again just tell her to enjoy all she can, and honor her poor father by believing that, wherever he may be now, he will be glad to know she is trying to be happy."

If the words held double solace no one could guess it by Dalton's manner. It was decidedly matter-of-fact above its tenderness. Joyce did not answer, except by a long sighing breath, but there was relief in its sound. Her hand still rested in the arm of her manager, and a feeling of safety and contentment gradually stole into her heart, often sore for her own loneliness, as well as over the woes of others.

CHAPTER XXI

IN THE LOCK-UP

The marshal unlocked the door of Nate's narrow cell and held his lantern aloft with a cheery, "Hello! Tierney. Brought you company, you see," and the prisoner rose slowly from his bunk, blinking and staring in the light, with an expectant air. It died out quickly, and murmuring in a broken voice,

"Oh, I thought it might be—evening, Mr. Dalton; evening, Miss," he looked helplessly around for a chair to offer Joyce.

The sheriff had brought one, which he placed for her, and Dalton braced himself against the wall, his hands in his pockets, while the officer sat down sociably beside his prisoner, on the bunk.

"Nate," said George, without preamble, "we don't want to pry into your affairs, nor trouble you in any way, but if we can help you we will be glad to—Miss Lavillotte and I. We believe you are man enough to wish to know the worst, without mincing, whatever it may be, and have come to tell you all. Your old chum, William Hapgood, is dead. The blow you gave him in your anger was harder than you meant. It crushed in his temple. He never knew what killed him.'
Nate looked up quickly.

"I didn't give him no blow, sir—not intentional, that is—I just swung the fire-stick in spite of me, and his head run agin it. I had been mad, but I'd got it under me. I'd dropped the stick to my side, and was goin' to lead him away, when Lucy's screech made me 'most crazy for a minute, and I didn't know rightly what I was doing. But 'twan't murder was in my heart. I'll swear to that! All I thought was to keep him off and see what ailded Lucy. It seemed so dumb queer to have her go fur me 'cause I was a-goin' to shet up her pa where he could cool off a bit! Women's queer cattle, though," he ruminated slowly, moving his head up and down.

Dalton shrugged his shoulders, then looked at Joyce and said gently,

"You mean we don't always understand them."

"Well, that's it, I s'pose. 'Twas going too fur, I presume, for me to say I'd take him to the lock-up. You see, that was a disgrace, and no mistake. It hurted her feelings an' then she turned agin me."

"But she let me bring a message," interposed Joyce quickly, though her manner was not assured. "I am certain she is sorry for you, and that she means to try and forgive you." Nate turned and looked at her several seconds, as if collecting his wits.

"It's sorter hard to understand," he said at last, in a hopeless tone. "I did it all for her—all but the part that I didn't do at all, for that was an accident and nothin' else—and she says she'll try to forgive me! I've heered of 'em pardoning men out o' state's prison after fifteen or twenty years, maybe, 'cause they found they'd never done the thing they was put in fur. *Pardoning* 'em out, mind you! I never could understand that. Seems as if it ought to be t'other way, but they go on doin' it just the same, so I s'pose I'm off on that, too. The fact is, things is pretty complexited sometimes. I can't get the right end, nohow."

"Nate," said Dalton, "do you claim you didn't mean to hit Hapgood—not at all?"

"Of course I didn't mean to. Hadn't I had him down, with the stick in my hand, right over him, and didn't I drop it, and take him by the collar, as easy as an old shoe, and tell him to come along?"

"But how, then"—began Dalton.

"Wait, sir, and I'll tell you straight."

Nate had risen and stood opposite the manager, his eyes glowing out from the yellow glare of the lantern, which was set on the floor in their midst. Joyce watched him from her chair, and the officer, also risen, leaned against the bunk, his gaze never leaving the speaker.

"'Twas this way. When Lucy called out so sharp, and come running out, I said 'twas to the lock-up I was going to take him. At that everybody screeched, and Bill turned on me like a mad bear. He's a gritty fighter"—He paused and looked around in his slow way—"I s'pose I oughter say was, now. Bill *was* a gritty fighter allays and he nearly knocked the breath outen me with his first blow. I felt the stick slidin' away from me, and knew 'twas my only holt. If Bill got the best o' me I was done fur. He was a mighty good fighter, and quicker'n a cat. I gripped at the stick and lost my balance, so't I nearly fell over backward. My arms flew out, spite of me, and the big stick struck wild. It killed poor Bill. But can't you see I didn't do it, Mr. Dalton? Before God, I ain't guilty of the murder of Lucy's father! I was mad, but not like that."

Dalton stepped forward and put out his hand.

"I believe you, Nate. I'm glad you told me!"

They shook hands warmly, and Joyce thrilled in sympathy.

The two talked a while longer, then all said good-night, but
not before Nate had been promised the best counsel money
could procure. As Joyce shook hands with him, Nate held
her soft fingers an instant, and looked searchingly into her
face, upon which the smoking lantern shed a fitful light.

"It's good of you to take so much trouble for me," he said.
"Did you come, 'cause Lucy asked you to?"

"Not exactly. I meant to come, anyhow, but was glad to
bring you word from her."

She felt she could not bluntly tell him that Lucy had avoided
speaking of him, especially when she was not at all certain as
to the girl's real feeling in the matter. But, alive to all the
suppressed wistfulness in the man's look and tone, she
yearned to comfort him, so said impulsively,

"Mr. Tierney, you must remember Lucy is terribly upset,
now. Her father lies there, dead by a cruel blow, and she
does not know that it was purely accidental. He may not
have been kind, but with all his faults he was her father. You
wouldn't think so much of Lucy if she forgot that. You'd
want her to think first of him, and the poor little orphaned
children."

"It's right you are, Miss!" grasping her hand heartily once
more. "She's a good girl, is Lucy, and does her duty, allays.
I'm glad she don't forget it now. But it 'most drives me mad
to be shut up here where I can't help her out any. She'll be

needing everything these days."

"She shall want for nothing, Nate. Mr. Dalton will tell you the Works are to pay Mr. Hapgood's funeral expenses, and continue his wages for the present. And we women, who are neighbors, will look after the dear girl in other ways. Don't worry about Lucy a minute! Just keep your mind clear to tell your story exactly as it is, and your acquittal is certain."

He looked down into her fair, upturned face and thought that even in the smudgy lantern's glow it looked like the face of some ministering angel. His own rugged visage worked with emotion. He could have kneeled to her, kissed her hand, touched the hem of her gown. But he only gave back her hand in a gentle manner, and said,

"Thank you, ma'am! I'll trust 'em all with you."

CHAPTER XXII

A VISIT TO LOZCOSKI

Joyce was called into the city by the Lozcoski affair the very next day. She was accompanied by George Dalton, also by a tablet filled with memoranda. There were things to buy for the Bonnivels, the Hapgoods, and for her own household. There was counsel to secure for Nate, some business to transact with Mr. Barrington, and, lastly, the Lozcoski matter. She could not expect anything but a busy, tiresome day. The gaunt, haggard face of the Pole haunted her by times, and in the train she suddenly remarked to her manager,

"I can't feel right over that Lozcoski! Every time I think of him I have a feeling that, somehow, he hasn't had fair play. There was an awful anger and despair in his look when he saw Murfree, and an awful terror met it. There has been wrong somewhere between those two men. You are sure the Pole had a fair trial?"

"Why, I suppose so. Of course he couldn't make himself understood very well without an interpreter, and they had difficulty in finding one—indeed had to give it up, I think—but there seemed no doubt of the matter."

"But why couldn't they find an interpreter?"

Fannie E. Newberry

"Well, as I understand it, the man comes from some remote part of the country, and speaks a villainous patois that even an educated person of his own land can scarcely make out. He is very ignorant, and slow to pick up our tongue."

"Was Murfree his only accuser?"

"Virtually. Still, his written deposition was so clear one could not gainsay it, I have heard."

"Written? Why did he not appear in court?"

"He was ill at the time, I believe. The fact is, it all happened once when I was east on business, and I really know but little about it, except from hearsay."

"Possibly this accounts for Lozcoski's anger against the man. Ignorant as he is, he has no sense of justice, perhaps. But he has suffered cruelly, and I can't help feeling that there is something he resents with all his soul."

"How imaginative you are! Don't you think all wrong-doers resent their punishment?"

"No, I do not. Many times in my life I have felt that I was not getting the full measure of my dues in that way. In fact, the hardest things in my experience have not come to me in the guise of reproof. I could not connect them with any of my ill doings. They just came out of a clear sky, as it were. Often, when I have been naughtiest, I have seemed to escape with less of pain and trouble than when I have been trying to be exceptionally good."

"Perhaps you were not logical enough to trace out cause and effect."

"Possibly not." She looked at him reflectively a moment. "I *am* very illogical, I fear. I once told myself that anything I might want to do to help Littleton would be over your dead body, almost. And, now, I never make a move without looking to you for the encouragement and support that make it perfectly satisfactory. I ought to have read you better from the first!"

Dalton rigidly suppressed the tremor of emotion that shook him from head to foot, and after an instant's pause answered in a cool tone,

"A man generally makes his employer's interests his own, doesn't he?"

She laughed sweetly.

"Am I your employer? It seems funny, doesn't it? But you need not try to explain it all away through your loyalty to my interests. I won't believe that. You are just as much interested in these people as I am. You know every man, woman, and child by name and nature—now 'fess! Don't you?"

"I'd be a chump if I did not make that a part of my business, at least to some extent. Of course I know some better than others."

They fell into silence after that. George had no desire to talk. It was enough to sit close beside a presence which meant the personification of purity and sweetness to him. Silence is never intrusive, She can sit between lovers, even, and shed a benediction upon both. It is only nervousness and fear that will drive her away. Joyce spoke first, in a tone almost of relief,

"Here we are! Now, shall we go first to Mr. Barrington?"

"When I have all these weightier matters off my mind I can better enjoy my feminine errands, I imagine."

"Certainly. And I hope we'll find him in."

He reached down her umbrella and followed her from the coach. The brakeman winked at the porter, and jerked a thumb towards them, as they walked leisurely down the platform.

"Best looking bride I've seen this season!" he remarked emphatically. "And the groom's got no eyes for any one else. Gee! Don't her clothes fit, though?"

"It's her figger fits," laughed the fat porter, with an unctuous chuckle. "Coffee sacks 'uld look well on her."

Mr. Barrington soon put them on the right path for their legal quest, and before noon they were following a turnkey along a dim stone corridor, which led to the hospital cell where Lozcoski was confined. A third party trailed respectfully in their rear. He was an interpreter whom Joyce had insisted upon securing, at a rather startling sum—for he was reported versed in every patois of Poland—that they might have an opportunity to converse freely with his countryman, before the latter was called upon to testify in the matter.

As the cell door opened before them a wild figure started up from the bunk, and stared through the gloom with great eyes. Joyce drew back, half startled, and Dalton spoke quickly, in a tone of authority.

"Bring this lady something to sit on outside here. She can't go in there."

A chair was brought, and he stood close beside her, repeating her low-toned requests aloud to the interpreter.

"Speak to him and tell him he has nothing to fear, that he is simply to tell an honest story of why he tried to fire the Works, and that all justice shall be granted him."

At first Lozcoski did not seem to listen. Crouched in an attitude of hopeless submission, he would not even raise his eyes as the interpreter's voice skipped over the hard consonants of his native tongue.

But presently his head was thrown back and he spoke in a quick, passionate tone. He was answered in a soothing voice, then took up the word himself, and getting well started, went on faster and faster, gradually straightening himself, and beginning to gesticulate with his hands. Once he raised the right hand and spoke low and impressively, while both he and the interpreter bowed their heads. With every sentence the latter's manner became more interested, and his short interrogations more eager. At last, as the narrative flowed on, he did not attempt to interrupt for some time, then he raised a hand, spoke a sentence in an authoritative manner, and turned to Dalton, seeming to think he was the person to whom he should defer.

"He tells a strange story, sir," said he in English, "and he has sworn to its truth by the most terrible oath in our religion. Shall I tell it to you now?"

"Yes, but speak low," said Dalton, looking towards Joyce, who nodded.

"It seems he, and the man who witnessed against him, both belong to the same secret society—a Nihilistic affair, I take it,—and are sworn to eternal brotherhood, of course. Once, this man he mentions was in danger of the law, and our prisoner here risked his life to save him. He does not explain all the details, but he was obliged to fly from Poland, and came to this country. Arrived here he tried various ways of making a living, and finally shipped as a sailor on a ship of war. He served for two months on the war-ship "Terror"— Joyce at this word looked up in startled fashion and turned pale—"but becoming disabled by a fall from the rigging, was left in hospital before its next cruise on the Florida coast. When he recovered sufficiently to be discharged he was told that a branch of his Nihilistic society was in this city, and would look after him, if he could get here. He managed to beat his way through, and was helped to work of various kinds for a month, or so. At length, one night at a meeting of the society, he encountered his old friend, and greeted him warmly. The man treated him well enough then, and they renewed their old intimacy, the other promising to find him a steady job at some big factory near by. His promises did not materialize, and our prisoner here appealed to him again and again, for he was destitute. Finally, at one of the monthly meetings, the old chum sought him out, and with a somewhat excited air said he was ready now to do him a service, if he would come along home with him that night. Our prisoner, who had been so exceptionally slow in acquiring the English language that he found it difficult to secure work anywhere, listened to his promises with much gratitude, and went along. The man took him to a small village surrounding some big works, and kept Lozcoski shut in his room through the whole of the next day, explaining that scab workmen were around and they must move carefully. That night the man roused him from sleep and told him to come along, for there was work for him at last. It was to be night work, but that was the best he could do for him. Suspecting no harm, he gladly went along and, directed by the other, was set to piling certain light trash against different parts of the building. The place was unlighted except by the glow of the furnaces inside, and he did not clearly know what he was doing. The other directed every movement, then left him standing in the deep shadow of an angle in the building, saying he would return in a moment. He was going after the boss. Lozcoski waited a long time. After a while there were loud shouts, and he could see that there was a glare all about him, as if of fire. He stepped out to see what had happened, and saw men running. Suddenly his chum sprang around the angle and caught him by the shoulder, pressing him forward. The men, at his call, turned and saw him. They were surrounded, and the chum talked loudly, and seemed denouncing our friend here. At any rate, they seized him and took him off to jail. He vainly tried to make some one comprehend the right and wrong of it, but could not make himself understood. Even the interpreter provided could not thoroughly understand him, and took his excited denunciations against the traitor as the ravings of one half insane with trouble. He does not rightly know, even yet, what he is imprisoned for, but his whole soul is bitter against that man, and he means to kill him yet, if it is the last thing he does on earth!"

George and Joyce looked at each other.

"You divined it," he murmured.

"Yes, to a certain extent. This Lozcoski must have justice, and so—so must Murfree."

"Yet you will hate to punish him, I can see!" His eyes, looking down into hers, were soft and shining, and held that little twinkle of tender ridicule which he seemed to reserve for her. She no longer resented it, however. She knew the loyalty that tempered it. She said in the same low tone,

"I want a question asked."

"The queen has but to command."

"Thanks, sir courtier. Ask who commanded that war-ship they spoke of."

Dalton turned to the interpreter, who put the question.

Lozcoski shook his head in replying, and the other explained, "He has forgotten."

"Then let him tell about the night he came to the Social-house," suggested the "queen," and the narrative was resumed.

It was not long. Lozcoski, while in prison, brooded over the wrong done him, day and night. When the fire gave him opportunity, he managed to escape with two other convicts, and leaving them at the first chance, he made his way to Littleton, resolving never to leave there until he had punished his man. He had chanced upon Dan's retreat, evidently, and had lived as he could for days, but on extremely short rations, as the fields were all harvested and berry time over. At night he would walk into town and wait around, hoping to see his victim. But the old man was wary and nearly always traveled in company. If Lozcoski had possessed a revolver he could have made short work of him, but having no means to procure any he had to wait for a personal encounter. The night he came to the Social-house he had been three days without food, and was insane with hunger. He had but two ideas in his disordered brain—to eat, and to kill. He must do the first in order to gain strength for the second. Even the actual sight of his enemy, before the door of the refreshment room, could not detain him from the food that he had caught sight of through the door. His hunger partly appeased, he had started out boldly to find Murfree, who fled for home on seeing him. Finding no one there, however, and afraid to be alone, he had rushed back again, feeling safety in numbers. He was just in time to meet his avenger in the hall, and in spite of the onlookers, the Pole's terrible onslaught had nearly finished him.

Dalton put several searching questions, then assuring the prisoner, through the interpreter, that matters should be righted, and his surroundings made comfortable at once, they left him with a new look on his worn face.

After leaving the interpreter, well satisfied with his morning's work, they were standing at a corner waiting for a trolley, when Joyce said in a weary voice,

"Is that all we have to do together?"

Dalton glanced down at her, and his lips twitched a little at the corners.

"For the present, I fear. Luncheon comes next, doesn't it? I had hoped—but I heard you accept Mr. Barrington's invitation to his house."

"Yes," absently. "Then I won't see you again?"

"What train did you think of taking for home?"

"I want to take the 5.13, if I can make it, but may have to wait for the 6.05. Which do you take?"

"I'll be there for the 5.13."

"All right!" cheerfully. "I'll try and be there. It's so much pleasanter to have company. Is this my car?"

He helped her on, and stepped back to await his own, going to another part of the city.

"Poor little thing!" he thought. "How the contact with crime sickens her. I can always see it. Yet she will not swerve from her good work, though she might sit lapped in luxury. They say those soldiers who sicken and tremble when going into the fight often make the bravest heroes. She is the pluckiest little fighter I ever saw, but it is herself she conquers—and me!"

CHAPTER XXIII

WAITING FOR THE TRAIN

It was a hard day for Joyce. Luncheon was late at Mr. Barrington's, and the purchases she must make took her far and near. It seemed impossible to get through for the 5.13 train; but she was somewhat astonished to find herself rushing from counter to counter, and eagerly consulting her little watch for fear she should miss it.

"But what if I do?" she asked herself. "I told them not to hurry dinner, and I can be at home soon after seven by the next train. What's the use in making myself ill by scrambling about like this?"

Yet, despite all arguing, as the moments fled her eagerness increased, and though she would not say, even to her own soul, "It is because George Dalton is taking that train," still something did say it within her, in utter disregard of her own proud disclaiming of any such motive. She even neglected one or two quite important purchases of her own, so that she might board a car for the distant depot with a minute or two of leeway, as she calculated.

But we have all heard about those plans that "go agley."

To her impatience the delays seemed endless, and she fairly anathematized herself, because she had not run a block or two to a cab-stand, and bidden one race the distance for double fare. Great trucks seemed determined to appropriate the rails and ignore all signals. At one place a jam of traffic stopped them entirely for a space. At a certain railway crossing they had to wait before the gates, Joyce in an ill-concealed agony of impatience, while a long freight train steamed slowly by. She felt half tempted to spring out and walk, then calmed herself with a contemptuous,

"How silly! I can take the next train. It will be tedious waiting, and no wonder I dread it, but I can buy something at the news-stand to read."

She scarcely waited for her car to stop when opposite the long, massive stone building, and, rushing through the great, ever-swinging doors, she traversed the office corridors with rapid tread, her hands too full of packages to consult her watch. But twisting her head to see the round clock, just above the entrance, with its great brass weights ponderously doling off the time, in plain view, she started with dismay, for its hands remorselessly pointed to fourteen minutes past five. One minute late. It was too provoking! She felt the tears close, and dashed on down the long steps leading to the passenger gates, at the risk of falling full length. She hoped against hope that some unprecedented event might have delayed the train. But as she sped along beside the cruel steel netting that shut her from the railway tracks, she realized that she was baffled. The one she was interested in was already pulling out from the end of the long depot. She could see it through the lace-work of steel, and knew every hope was gone. She must calm herself and wait. But she could not refrain from watching it a moment, with hungry eyes, pressed like a child's against the barrier. It was carrying George home, and she was left behind! She felt like a deserted waif, and looked it. Somebody, watching the little pantomime from behind a baggage truck not far away, read in the gaze almost more than he dared to believe.

"Her disappointment is not on your account, you booby!" he told himself frankly. "Don't be an idiot."

Joyce turned sadly, wearily, towards the waiting-room.

Her drooping figure, so unlike her usual erect and joyous bearing, proclaimed her dejection, as well as fatigue.

She felt utterly spent.

She had not reached the room when a hand lightly touched her shoulder. She turned quickly to meet George Dalton's smiling gaze, and her own face amply reflected his gladness. As he saw it a new expression leaped to his eyes. They were brilliant—were they triumphant, too? But he controlled himself to speak in an even, sensible tone.

"Let me take your packages. You are loaded down."

"Oh, it is you?" cried Joyce, catching her breath. "You didn't take the train then? Were you late, too?"

"I couldn't seem to get away, somehow," he answered with nonchalance, heaping the packages up methodically on one arm, and avoiding her glance. "But we've plenty of time for the next," laughing mischievously. "Can you stand it to wait an hour?"

"I'll have to, won't I?" But she did not look oppressed by the anticipation, he could see.

"We'll try and mitigate its horrors," he remarked as they

slowly mounted the stairs. "I'll secure the best rocker the room affords, and all the periodicals on the stand, if you say so."

"Oh, must I read?" she cried naively. "I thought we might talk, perhaps."

He looked away suddenly. He dare not meet her softened gaze just then.

"We will do whatever you wish," he said in a steady tone, after a minute. "Now, let's see."

They had reached the room, and he took a calm survey of it, in all its details. Then he marched up to a small urchin who, with much effort, was rocking a large chair to and fro, his chubby legs just reaching to the edge of its broad seat.

"I'm afraid you are working too hard, my son," he remarked blandly. "Just take these pennies, and drop them in the slot of that machine over in the farthest corner—see? There's no knowing what will drop out in return."

"I know!" cried the youth all agrin. "It's butter-scotch, or gum. I've seed that kind before."

He toddled briskly off with the handful of pennies and Dalton drew the vacated chair into a quiet nook, where the light fell softly and the crowd did not gather.

"Follow! Follow!" he called in a low tone over his shoulder, and, smiling happily, Joyce obeyed.

He seated her, heaped her many parcels on a convenient marble slab near by, then stood and looked at her a moment.

"I think you'll do," he observed in a whimsical tone, "but

there's one thing more."

"Yes, a chair for you," she returned eagerly.

His bronzed cheek took on a perceptible tinge of red.

"Thank you! I would not mind sitting on the floor, I think—just there," and his tan toe lightly touched a spot just beyond the edge of her gown. "But, for custom's sake, I'll find a chair. We are not Turks, you see."

He strode away quite out of sight, but after some time returned, dragging an arm chair over the tiling. In his other hand he gingerly held a quaint little Indian basket, gaily stained, and inwoven with sweet-scented grass. It was heaped with great yellow peaches, each with a crimson cheek, while, flung carelessly among them, were clusters of grapes in their perfection, purple-blue and whitish-green, promising rare sweetness and flavor.

"They were the best I could find, but scarcely good enough for you," he remarked deprecatingly, as he placed the basket in her hand.

"Oh, beautiful! What delicious fruit! And where did you ever find such a pretty, fragrant basket?"

"Have you never noticed the old squaw, who sits mutely amid her wares near the traffic gate? She declared this her choicest creation, her masterpiece, indeed. I am so glad you admire it!"

"The whole thing is lovely. It makes me hungry to look at this fruit, and yet it seems too pretty, just as it is, to spoil by dipping into it."

Fannie E. Newberry

He laughed and, selecting the largest peach of all, began to pare it with his own pocket-knife, making a plate and napkin of his newspaper. With careful slowness he pared and stoned and quartered it, then handed her the segments on a bit of the paper torn from a clean spot.

"Such immense pains!" she laughed, as she received the offering.

"It is very little I can do for you," he murmured in return, and looked off through the window, though nothing but an expanse of unlighted brick wall could be found beyond.

Joyce did not answer. She ate her fruit slowly, as if luxuriating in its taste. Presently she looked up.

"And won't you eat any of my peaches?" she asked archly, with a lingering emphasis on the "my."

"Indeed I will!" reaching with eager haste for the one she offered.

She had selected the finest one left and, as his fingers touched it, she clung to it an instant.

"So you *will* take a peach from me?" she said, with an odd expression; "Especially after being the one to secure it to me."

"Oh yes, with pleasure."

"I'm glad your pride has limits," laughing and flushing a little. "Some people are proud over everything."

"I am proud over seeing you enjoy my little gift."

"And I am proud over being the recipient of your gift, which strikes me as not being so 'little' as you seem to think it. After all, this matter of giving and taking should be very simple; don't you see? The surcharged cloud pours its electricity into the empty one, and both are equalized. But has the full cloud any more to boast of than the other?"

He smiled.

"I think I never saw any one so ingenious in pleas for the sharing system. Possibly, if you were the empty cloud you would feel differently."

"I hope not. I think it takes a larger nature to receive nobly than to give nobly."

"So do I. It takes a nature so great few men have attained to it," he said quickly. "I acknowledge that I have not."

"'A fault confessed is half redressed'," murmured Joyce.

"*Is* pride a fault?" he asked quickly.

"Isn't it? According to the Bible it's a large one, almost a crime." Her laughing eyes sought his, and she continued, "Now, I haven't a particle of pride. I've eaten one peach and I want another. Moreover, I want it pared and quartered."

They were almost as isolated in their little corner as if in a nook of the woods. The crowds surged to and fro, and its units were "but as trees walking" to their oblivious eyes. Joyce was discovering new depths in George Dalton's nature. He was a thinker, and as his thinking had grown out of contact with men, rather than from grubbing in books, it was often of a unique and picturesque kind.

Fannie E. Newberry

He saw the ludicrous in everything, and, with all his practicality, there was a strain of romance so fresh and young mingled with it, that it made a boy of him whenever he was dominated by it. He was the boy to-night, and as he leaned towards Joyce, talking in an undertone, his eye bright, his laughter frequent, his manner full of respectful friendliness, she forgot that he had ever seemed hard, cold, and given over to business alone.

At length the call of a train at some distant doorway startled Joyce, and she glanced around.

"Isn't that our train he's calling? It can't be! But I'm afraid it is."

Each consulted a watch, and looked guiltily at the other.

"It has been very short," said Joyce involuntarily.

"And very sweet!" added George below his breath. "Well, come on, little parcels. One-two-three-four—have I got them all? Why—what is it?"

The girl's face had a piteous look as it was turned to his.

"I had forgotten it all—the Hapgoods, Lozcoski, poor Nate! We were as easy as if there were no trouble anywhere. It all rushed over me once more, and I felt, for the instant, that I could never bear it again. But you will help me? You'll understand now, and not think me foolish and crazy, as you sometimes do?"

"Do I? I did not know it. I'll stand by you in everything, never fear! Come, child, or we'll miss this train, too."

She preceded him without a word, and he was glad to keep

quite behind for a little, for when he remembered how he had called her "child" his face was hot with embarrassment. He had never forgotten before. Had she noticed? Her face told him nothing.

As they hurried out through the gates and down the platform to their waiting train, the passengers were descending from another, just arrived. Hastily crossing this tide transversely two men, arm in arm, passed them close in the busy throng.

There was a familiar look about one of them, Joyce thought, as she had just a side glimpse while hurrying by. But, absorbed in her own haste, she did not notice particularly. George stopped short and turned for an instant, then kept on just behind her. He had recognized Nate, and knew him to be in charge of an officer, doubtless being conveyed to the county jail. He had not expected this event till morning, and had meant, himself, to prepare the poor fellow for it. Saddened and angry that the man had been so summarily dealt with, Dalton's face took on its sternest look, which Joyce caught as they seated themselves.

Not knowing its cause, she was startled and chagrined at the change. What had she said, or done, to cause it?

Silently ruminating amid the sweet experiences of the day she failed to find any clue, till he at length said, with a sigh.

"I have something to tell you. I thought at first I would keep it to myself, but I'd rather tell you, myself, than have you hear it elsewhere. They've taken poor Nate away. Did you notice, just now—"

"Was that he—with the tall man arm in arm? And was the tall man an officer?"

Fannie E. Newberry

George nodded to both questions.

"Yes, I'm sorry to say."

"Oh, poor Nate. He will be heart broken. Why couldn't they have left him there? Till after the funeral at least. Oh, my friend, we have been too thoughtless to-day! Our people at home have been suffering."

"And, had you been the sufferer, would you begrudge others a bit of joy?"

"No, no, indeed!"

"Then why be self-reproachful now? We have done what we could for them, and that is all even they could ask. We will not spoil the day with regrets, or self-upbraidings, now."

He spoke in a deep voice, and added hesitantly, after a moment,

"I have not had so much happiness, myself, but that I am greedy of it. This day will stand out from all the days of my life. On it you, Joyce Lavillotte, called me, George Dalton, friend!"

CHAPTER XXIV

NIGHT WATCHERS

The funeral of William Hapgood was over. Death had dignified him, and few ventured to speak of him as "Bill," just now. Lucy had wept convulsively in her very long and very black veil, and Tilly and Rufie had sniveled on either side of her, after a last shrill quarrel over which should wear the black jacket, and which the cape with a black ribbon bow, that Joyce had provided.

The whole village had attended the obsequies at the pretty new church, and favorably commented thereon. Mrs. Hemphill thought it a "turrible waste" that they did not have the silver name-plate taken off the casket, however, and declared solemnly:

"Them that buries silver's like to dig fur copper 'fore they die theirselves."

But the women were all deeply impressed with Lucy's genteel mourning costume, and felt an added respect for the little creature in her trailing crepe. Marie and Babette were in and out continually, aiding and suggesting, and Rachel had stayed with Lucy every night.

Fannie E. Newberry

During one of these she and Babette had been asked to "sit up with the corpse," Gus Peters and Dan being chosen to share their vigil. It had taken much urging to induce Dan to feel it his duty, but at last he had given in with a good grace, and appeared with Gus promptly at the appointed hour. With these people a funeral was often the forerunner of a wedding. It was quite the proper thing for those "keeping company" together to sit out the long night hours beside the dead, and too often a keg of liquor was tapped, over which hilarity reigned to a ghastly degree.

There was no danger of that in this case, though. Neither Gus, nor Dan, was of the drinking set, and Lucy had a horror of the stuff, so would not have it in the house. All was decorum over the body of the man who had been ruined by his own appetite.

They sat around the fire the cool fall evenings required, and talked in low tones. Once in a while one or another of the boys would step into the little room off, a minute, then come quietly back to the group. Bill Hapgood had good care that night. But after a time the little group seemed to disintegrate into pairs. Gus and Babette, sitting side by side on the old lounge, dropped their voices to whispers, while Dan and Rachel, somewhat withdrawn from each other, slowly rocked in two old cane chairs. As Dan returned to his seat after one of his short absences with the dead, he flung a glance toward the other couple and remarked, sotto voce.

"Gus is getting lots of cheek since he come to be an architect. There was a time he darsn't look at Bab."

"He always liked her, though."

"Oh, of course. Who don't? She's pretty and good and gay. But she felt above Gus, once."

"Did she? I never thought so."

"*He* thought so. She would hardly notice him."

"Sometimes," said Rachel slowly, "folks feel offish themselves, and imagine everybody else does. I've heard Freda
Wilkes talk about folks slighting her, when she'd go along
the street with her head so high they couldn't anybody reach
up to her. I'm some that way myself, mother says. But I don't
know it till it's over. I get to thinking, and forget what's
around me. It seems to me, often, as if there was a lot more
things in this world—yes, and people too—than we can see
around us. I don't believe in ghosts, either, at least not the
scarey kind, but sometimes I seem to get off this earth into
something higher and better. It's then I forget folks. But it
isn't pride. I never feel how little and ignorant I am as at
those times."

Dan rocked on silently and looked at the fire.

He loved to hear Rachel talk. There was a peculiar cadence in
her voice, a rich depth, unusual in young women. There was
not a shrill nor common strain in it. That "high" look Joyce
had noted went with high thoughts, and a voice undertoned by
a beautiful soul. Dan felt this without thinking it out in so
many words. Another idea began to force its way into his
moody brain. Just because Rachel had this unusual quality,
this power of looking inward, might she not understand the
complexities of his life better than others? He wondered in his
tense silence, but did not raise his eyes to see.

His silence finally chilled Rachel, and she, too, began to
stare at the fire. The low talk of the other couple ceased and
Gus said, explanatorily,

"We were just speaking of Mr. Dalton and Miss Lavillotte.

Bab thinks that'll be a match."

"She's good enough for a king," said Babette, "and as pretty and grand as a princess, and he is our king here. Why shouldn't it be all right?"

"She's different from him, though," returned Rachel slowly. "She's been brought up different, Mr. Dalton has made himself a gentleman, but she didn't have to be made. She is a lady born."

"She must have money, too," said Gus. "She's real generous, I hear; and I guess it's true, for I know she has a kind way with her."

"I don't know about her having much money," said Rachel, "but she seems to feel that we all belong to her, somehow, and that she's got to look after us. If the Works, and the whole town, too, was her own she couldn't be more interested."

"She consults lots with Dalton," spoke up Dan. "But they say they're connections of some kind, and he looks after what property she's got."

"Then she has means?" asked Babette.

"Must have considerable," replied Gus. "That old fellow that works for her told me, once, that if she wanted to she could make a big splurge, but she wouldn't do it. He hinted as if she had reasons for being so interested here, but I couldn't pump a thing out of him. I guess he likes to boast pretty well, and he thinks she made the earth, anyhow."

"It's queer," mused Rachel, "that the new boss has never appeared in all these changes and improvements. I should think he'd want to see for himself what's going on. If he cares enough to do so much, he ought to care enough to come and look on."

"But he's in Europe, ain't he?"

"What makes you think so, Dan?"

"I asked Mr. Dalton, once, if he'd be here before we put in the new annealing furnace, just to see what he'd say, and he answered that he thought not. It would be a long time before young Early would reach these shores. So I concluded he was across the water."

"You didn't like Miss Lavillotte at first, did you, Rachel?" asked young Peter.

The girl laughed out, a low laugh in deference to the dead.

"Yes, I liked her so well I tried not to notice her! I expected she'd do something high and mighty to make me mad, so I held myself back. But I found I didn't need to. I was soon ashamed of it. She can't help looking different from others. A china cup isn't to blame for looking finer and whiter than a brown jug. It's made so!"

"Speaking of cups and jugs makes me hungry, somehow," observed Gus, glancing about him.

"Didn't they say something about a lunch for us, Bab?"

"Yes, it's all fixed there in the cupboard. Want me to make you a cup of coffee? You know I can make good coffee, Gus."

Babette could not help being coquettish, even amid solemn

surroundings at two o'clock in the morning. As she spoke she glanced sidewise at the young man and tossed back her pretty curling locks from her forehead. In a few minutes the coffee-pot was slowly steaming over the little gas grate, a delicious odor beginning to exude from its spout.

The girls, with quiet movements, drew a small table before the hearth, and set out thereon cold meat, bread, and milk, also the inevitable pie of the Americanized workman. The boys helped them, or pretended to, and even Dan grew sociable under the sense of close companionship and good cheer.

They had finished their impromptu meal, but were still at the table, thoroughly enjoying themselves, half forgetful of the awesome figure in the next room, when out of the weird stillness came a sudden cry, and a dull thud, as of some body falling against a solid obstruction.

Babette clutched at Gus, while Dan's hand involuntarily closed over Rachel's, outstretched in terror. Then, ashamed of the momentary start, he drew it away and rose from his chair.

"Sit still," he said, "till I look into this."

He stepped into the little room, Gus at his heels, but both turned back at once, assured all was right there.

"It's outside," said Dan, in a low voice. "Some drunken man, probably. You stay with the girls, and I'll go out and see."

"Not much," said Gus indignantly. "Guess I'm no more afraid than you are!"

He had no idea of appearing cowardly before the girl of his

heart. But she clung to him.

"Oh Gus, I'm scared to death! Don't go."

Dan had already let himself out, bidding Rachel lock the door behind him. She turned now to Babette.

"Come, come, Bab!" she said. "We are not going to be nervous and frighten the children."

She was interrupted by a shriek, long and blood-curdling. The girls clung together, and Gus rushed out after Dan, fearing something terrible had occurred. A frightened cry from upstairs was almost a relief from the strain, and the girls fled back to the stairway door to meet Lucy and the little girls, who were huddled there in a great fright.

"What is it?" they asked in a whispered chorus. "Is pa all right?"

Rachel was the only one calm enough to answer.

"Some drunken fellow, likely. Come out by the fire, girls, or you'll take cold. Dan has gone to see about it."

"And Gus," added Babette jealously, finding her voice to defend her lover.

They all crouched together before the fire, Rachel bringing a shawl to wrap around the scantily clad sisters, and the five enlarged upon the event in all its details, as people do whose range of thought is not wide. The morning twilight was gray in the room when a noise outside caught their attention.

"Dan! I know his step," cried Rachel in a joyous tone, springing to open the door.

Lucy and the children fled to shelter behind the stairway door, and remained there to hear without being seen. Dan stumbled in with an exhausted air, and dropped into a chair.

"Hasn't Gus come?" he asked.

"No, where is he?" cried Babette excitedly. "You didn't leave him alone with the thing, did you?"

Dan smiled.

"The 'thing', as you call it, was poor old Murfree. He got out of bed while the nurse was asleep, and has been wandering around enough to kill a well person. I did not know who I was following for a long time, for sure, but I suspected it was Murfree when I saw he was undressed. He led me an odd chase, I tell you!"

"Oh, tell us all about it!" piped up Tilly from the stairway.

Dan looked towards it, then broke into a laugh, perhaps the first real mirthful sound that had passed his lips since his brother's death. It made Rachel's heart beat faster with joy and surprise.

"All right!" he said. "I will. It don't seem like a sick man could do it, but he did. He struck out for the Works as soon as I got outside and I after him. Didn't you hear him shriek. He was quite a ways ahead, and I let him keep so. Soon as I was sure about him I knew I oughn't to frighten him by waking him too sudden."

"Why, was he asleep?" This from Rufie.

"Sure! But what he did was the queerest. He began dodging in and out around the sheds, and every now and then he'd stoop and seem to be fixing something. Then he'd motion like he was lightin' a match. I kept back and watched him. I knew by this time he was either doing over something he'd done before which had come to him in a dream, or else somebody had hypnotized him. He moved just like a machine. I kept thinking he'd drop, for it seemed as if he must be worn out, but he didn't for a long time."

"But where was Gus all this while?" asked Babette.

"I don't know. I think he went some other way. I didn't see him again till Murfree had led me along opposite of Dodge's cow-shed. As long as the man was making for home I wouldn't disturb him. But right there what I expected happened. He fell in a dead faint. And just then, mighty luckily for me, Gus came up. We couldn't manage him alone, so we called up Jim Dodge out of bed, and he helped us get him into the house. Everybody was out hunting Murfree up, so we had to stay till I could call Dr. Browne by 'phone and we could get him warmed up once more. I left Gus there, to come and tell you, for I knew you'd worry. I guess this night'll finish poor old Tonguey Murfree! Queer, wasn't it?"

He was looking at Rachel, and she answered, thrilling to the naturalness of his look and tone, after these weary months of deepest gloom and silence. The old Dan seemed to have come back to her out of the long, gruesome night. She understood, without explanation, that these adventures had taken him out of himself, that care and thought for others had lifted him above the murk of his own despair. He was as alert, interested, and ready to talk, as ever he used to be. As she plied him with questions she longed in some tangible way to show her quickened sympathy and gladness. She wanted to clasp his hand, to touch his arm, to smile up into his eyes. But she was proud; and then she feared to break the happy spell.

Instead, she set the coffee over, and when it had boiled, brought it to his side.

"I know you're tired and hungry, Dan. I'll fix you up a cup that will make you fresh again. You like just a little milk, I know, but plenty of sugar. And here's the last piece of pie."

Rachel was true to the traditions of her class. She knew the way to a man's heart. Dan ate and drank, feeling that some barrier was down between them. This was not the Rachel of yesterday, who without seeming to repulse him, yet held herself so high and far he dare not believe in her kindness, even. Was it his hand that had swept that barrier away? Yet he had sworn never to do that while the memory of his brother stood between them, for he firmly believed that Rachel had been Will's promised wife.

CHAPTER XXV

CAMILLE SPEAKS OUT

"There's George Dalton going to Joyce's again," remarked Camille, turning from the library window which looked towards the other house. "They seem to find plenty of matters to discuss, lately."

"I can well believe it," replied her mother calmly. "What with hurrying to complete all the houses before snow falls, and looking after Nate's trial and Lucy's family, it keeps Joyce on the anxious seat."

"Oh well, she likes it," laughed the girl. "There, he's gone in now. He always comes to the house to talk nowadays, instead of her going to the office."

"It's a better plan, I think."

"You always think everything is either good, better, or best, mother. But it seems to me—"

She stopped to study the Madame's sightless countenance, until that lady asked, laughingly,

"Well, what has cut you off, child? I imagine you suspended in mid-air."

Camille joined in the laugh, but not too heartily.

"I was going to say, it seems to me there's something more than business in it all, ma mere."

Madame Bonnivel looked up quickly.

"Are you justified in saying that, daughter?"

"I don't know. I only spoke of the way in which it strikes me. There now! He's coming out, and Joyce with him. She has on her new jacket and her best walking hat. I do verily believe they are going into the city. And I was going myself this afternoon, then gave it up—how provoking! She looks odd, Joyce does."

"How, odd?"

"Well, excited perhaps. She doesn't seem to see, or think, of anything but just what she is doing. I wonder if anything has happened, or if it's just being with him?"

"Camille, dear, is it quite the thing to stand and comment on your neighbor, so?"

"Why, it's only Joyce, mother. And I won't any longer. She's out of sight now, anyway, and gone straight toward the station, too. But, I will maintain, she consults twice as much with that manager lately as with you, mother. You know that as well as I do."

A slight contraction of the Madame's smooth brow proved that the shaft had hit.

"Yes, that is probable enough. It isn't to be wondered at, either. He is her manager, and an excellent one. Camille, did you say Leon enclosed a note to Joyce in his last letter to you?"

The girl's face broke into a mischievous grin. "What made you think of that just now, dear? Yes he did, but it was a short one, and she didn't show it to me. I wish he would come home!"

The Madame sighed.

"So do I. After all, what prospects in life has a naval officer without private property? He must always be gone from home, where he may be exposed to unknown dangers. He can scarcely hope to form family ties."

"Humph! Joyce's husband needn't be in the navy, if she doesn't like to have him, mother."

"Hush, child, don't be absurd! They are like brother and sister."

"But they are not brother and sister, and I'm glad of it—if that Dalton will keep his distance. I don't know but it's my duty to make up to him, myself."

"Camille! Don't be coarse."

"Coarse! You ought to hear most of the girls talk. Well, good-by. I told Joyce I'd go and tend library this afternoon, and I must be off. I'll send Dodo in to keep you out of mischief."

She stooped to kiss the smooth cheek, where time had been sparing of wrinkles, and her mother drew her down for a

Fannie E. Newberry

closer caress.

"Adieu, my love. One of the lessons my blindness teaches me is that, a great many times in this world, the hardest work we are given is just to sit one side and neither speak, nor act. It is then prayer becomes an unspeakable blessing."

"Mother, you're awfully good! I won't meddle; don't worry. Here's Dodo. She hasn't learned that lesson yet, bless her heart! Now don't let Mamma mope, Blossom."

"Me'll tate tare ob her, S'e tan p'ay wiv mine Wobin, an' hol' mine dolly."

Camille disappeared, throwing kisses as she went. The library she mentioned was one in connection with the school, and somewhat chaotic in condition. Joyce had bought a selected lot of good reading matter in paper covers, with which to start a circulating library, and with the assistance of the Bonnivels, was getting it in shape. In the absence of a catalogue the books were now numbered on the backs, and when issued the corresponding number, on a slip of paper marked the vacant place on the shelf. In addition, the name of the drawer had to be recorded, making the work of distribution something of a task. As yet no regular librarian had been appointed. Joyce thought that either Dan or Rachel could do the work satisfactorily, but both were valuable glass-workers, and Dalton demurred at giving up any of their time. So the matter rested.

Though well into the Fall the day had come off sunny and mild. As always, in such weather, that part of the population not confined in the factory was pretty well turned out of doors. Camille, crossing the park from one end to the other, noted the women standing about in groups, or passing from cottage to cottage, and wondered when they ever found time for their household duties. She exchanged pleasant nods with those she met—all liked her gay, gypsyish face and easy manners—and was in great good humor when the school-house was reached.

It was still early and the children not dismissed, but already a large group of women were waiting in the library room. Among these, so demure and still as to seem oldest of all, waited Lucy Hapgood. Camille could scarcely keep back a smile at sight of her incongruous attire. Her gown was a cotton one of a washed out indigo-blue, with large polka spots that had once been white, before the other color had beclouded them. Over this, as if apologizing and condoning, streamed the sombre veil, more suitable for a widow than for that round-faced child. But Lucy drew it about her with a tender touch, as she sat apart, and Camille could plainly note her satisfaction in its heavy folds.

The latter at once began her work of distribution, that these older people might be disposed of before the school children should come trooping in. When Lucy's turn arrived, and she took her place before the little railing, like a veiled oriental mute, Camille looked down upon her with an air of good comradeship, and said,

"I know you'll want something bright and wide awake. I don't believe you like doleful books any better than I do."

Lucy's demure face lightened, but she seemed to hesitate for a reply.

"I did like that kind," she said finally, "but now I don't know. Mis' Hemphill said I ought to read something sober, nowadays. There's a book about a girl that was took up because they thought she'd killed her father, and they tried to torment and torture her into telling."

"Good gracious! Such a book would be the death of you. Is she crazy? I'll pick you out something. Now, here's the loveliest story! It's about two merry, sensible girls who found themself obliged to earn their own living. They did not sit down and cry, but just went about it, as gay and jolly as you please, and they had lots of funny adventures, but conquered in the end. I know you'd like it."

Lucy looked at the volume wistfully.

"Do you think I ought to?" she whispered.

"Of course I do. Why not? Look it over, at least."

She took the book, dipped into it here and there, looked at the illustrations, then glanced up with a flushing cheek.

"I know I'd like it and, if you say so—"

"Certainly I say so. What's its number?"

"One hundred and twenty."

"All right. Now, you read every word of it, and tell me how you like it when you bring it back, will you?"

Lucy tucked it carefully under her veil, but lingered.

"Isn't Miss Lav'lotte going to be here to-day?"

"No, I think she went into the city, probably to see Mr. Nate Tierney."

Camille spoke deliberately, turning to replace a volume in the large pine case as she did so.

"Do—do you know where 'tis she goes to see him?" asked the girl in a low voice, glancing about her with a furtive air.

Camille looked at her quickly.

"Don't you know? Haven't they told you?'"

"Then he is in—jail?"

Camille nodded regretfully.

"I kinder thought maybe Mr. Dalton might get him out," was the next remark in a despairing tone.

"I hope they will soon, Lucy, but it takes time. Have you been to see him yet?"

"I?" Lucy started, and stared at her.

"Yes, you to be sure. He has been such a good friend of yours. Of course they'll do all they can—Mr. Dalton and Joyce—but you know him so much better he could tell you things he wouldn't them. Then, he must get awfully lonely for his own friends. He suffers terribly over it all."

"But—but—you know what he's in jail for?"

"Of course. But nobody believes he is guilty. Miss Lavillotte says, and so does every one, that it was just an accident."

"He was mad at pa, though, fearful mad!"

"Yes, he owns to that. But he had gotten control of himself. He simply meant to shut him up where he could not harm you."

Lucy sighed.

"I wish I was sure. Nate never lied to me in his life. If he'd say it solemn and true I'd believe it."

"Why don't you go to see him, then, and ask all about it?"

"Oh, I couldn't What would people say?"

She shrank back as if from a blow.

"Do you always stop to think about that?" asked Camille with contempt. "Why don't you figure out what is really right and then go ahead? I do."

Lucy studied her a minute, then asked in return,

"Do you think it's right to care more for other folks than for your own family?"

"I don't think it's natural, but, if you do, there must be something wrong with the family. We generally like those nearest to us, if they'll let us."

"Yes, that's so," said the other eagerly, as if new light were coming to her.

"As far as family is concerned, though, I like Joyce Lavillotte better than any cousin I have, almost better than my own sister, and she is no relation at all."

"Isn't she?"

"Not the slightest. And my mother, I do believe, likes her better than anybody in the world."

"Not better'n you—her own girl?"

"Just as well, I'm sure. And it's all right, too. I would not have it otherwise. They say this Mr. Tierney has always been kindness itself to you and the children; I should think you ought to love him just as well as if he were your big brother."

"Do you think so—really?"

"I know it."

Something of perplexed sadness fell away from the child's face, and just then the measured beat of young feet being marched through the halls proclaimed that school was dismissed. Lucy turned quickly and grasped at Camille.

"Say, I don't know where to go nor how to get at him. I don't know where to write to him, even. If you'd tell Miss Lav'lotte, don't you b'lieve she'd go with me, or something? She's so kind."

"Of course she would. I'll tell her."

"And see here, you—you won't tell anybody else?" speaking low and hurriedly for the children were at the door.

"Tell! Of course not! But Lucy, what ails you is you have been so used to care and sorrow that you don't dare to catch the least ray of sunshine that comes to you. Now, that's all wrong. You ought to talk with my mother. Come and see us some day, on the knoll, will you? Come soon."

"Oh may I? How lovely to ask me!" Lucy's face fairly shone at the thought. "Good by," she whispered, fairly squeezing Camille's little brown paw, "good-by. I'll come, sure," and dropping the thick veil to hide smiles rather than tears, she glided out between the ranks of impatient children, who looked after her with awed interest.

That evening Camille, full of frank curiosity, tripped across to the other house, tapping lightly on the side door opening upon the driveway, and entered without waiting for admission. The room she stepped into was unlighted, except from the hall beyond, but crossing both she came into a delightful little apartment, softly illumined with lamps which shed a rosy light through their silken shades. A couple of logs burned on the brass andirons of the fireplace with an aromatic odor that suggested deep pine woods.

Before them a couch was drawn, upon which Joyce nestled lazily amid a nest of pillows. At a table, little withdrawn, Ellen was reading aloud from a late magazine, the rosy light making her look almost young and handsome to-night. She withdrew, after a word or two of greeting, while Joyce without stirring, said drowsily,

"I know you won't ask me to get up, Camille; you are too good-natured. Come, take this easy little rocker and tell me all you know."

"No thank you. I've come to put you to the question, my lady! Who told you you could go off to the city with that handsome George Dalton when I had given up the trip just because I hated to go alone?"

"Had you? What a pity we did not know!" The lamps made Joyce's cheeks a lovely color. "Of course our business would have been a bore to you, but we could have met for a nice time somewhere, later."

"How do you know it would have been a bore? And what was 'our' business, anyhow?"

"Camille, we are both convinced that poor Lozcoski has been unjustly accused, and Murfree is the real criminal. To get the Pole out of prison, and to keep Murfree out, requires some man[oe]uvring, and a lot of 'lawing,' as Gilbert calls it."

"But why keep that old Murfree out? I should think he deserved all he can get."

"I suppose he does, but the poor man is so ill. It's a cruel world, dear—but a beautiful one, too!"

"Then, didn't you go to see the Tierney man?" asked Camille, more interested in that tragedy than the other.

"Yes, we did. He has every comfort, and we secured him the best of counsel. We are sure he will be acquitted."

Camille winked at the fire, a smile on her lips. That "we" tickled her. She glanced around at Joyce, who lay dreamily gazing into the blaze, her eyes and thoughts far away. She broke into a little laugh which attracted the dreamer's attention, and as the latter turned her head surprisedly, she said.

"Do you realize how funny that 'we' and 'our' sound, Joycie dear? Six months ago you thought little enough of George Dalton, and now he is in everything you do."

"Well, it's his business to be, child. Six months ago I did not understand nor appreciate him—now, I do."

Camille gave a grunt.

"We don't see anything of you at all, any more," she flung out, almost spitefully.

"I have been very busy, sweetheart. Did you eat pickled peppers for supper? I wouldn't. They spoil your—complexion."

Camille had to laugh at the tone of this, and at the other's merry eyes.

"No, I didn't, and I've been good all day. I went to your old library concern and attended to it beautifully, and I talked to Lucy like a grandmother, and gave her splendid advice. She really chirked up wonderfully, and tried to hide her smiles behind that ridiculous veil. Isn't she funny?"

"Or pathetic—which? But you've been a good child, I see. Now, try the same process on me. I'm all tired out and need 'chirking,' too."

"You may be tired, but it hasn't struck in, Joyce. You're just beaming inside, and it shines through."

Joyce laughed and snuggled down closer into her pillows.

"What sharp eyes you have! So you don't approve of me unless I am weary inside, as well as out?"

"I do too, only—well, this is just the way you used to look when we were expecting Leon home, and we are not expecting him now."

"Oh, you think I have mistaken the occasion? I see!" She spoke in a tone Camille knew of old which, though seldom used towards a Bonnivel, could hold almost any one in check. So the girl went on rapidly, determined to have her say out,

"I won't beat about the bush any more. I believe you are

perfectly happy with George Dalton, and don't want anybody else. Now, aren't you? Own up!"

Joyce had burrowed so deeply by this time that only one pink ear was visible, and Camille was looking at this with a determined expression when a quick, firm step was heard in the hall—in fact, more than one—and Larry's voice called impatiently.

"Where are you girls, anyhow? Can't you let a wanderer in without the ceremony of an announcement?"

"Here!" called Camille rising, while Joyce hastily shook up the pillows and arranged her hair. "What's wanted of us?"

"Very little," cried Larry, bouncing in with a beaming face. "I've simply brought you a new beau," and he pointed behind him to a tall, straight figure in dark blue, which stood at "attention," smiling happily.

"Leon!" cried Camille, springing to his arms, and Joyce was thankful for the instant's space in which to collect herself.

When he turned quickly to her both hands were out to meet his own, but she neither paled nor flushed as her eyes met his with a glance of truest friendship and camaraderie.

Fannie E. Newberry

CHAPTER XXVI

NOT WELCOME

They visited long that evening, and Joyce slept late the next day. When she arose Ellen hastened to inform her that Lucy Hapgood had telephoned to ask when she might call and talk with her a few moments, and that Mr. Dalton was below, waiting for a certain architect's drawing Joyce had wished him to see, but would not let her be disturbed till she awoke of her own accord.

"I told him, if 'twas just a drawin' that I'd bring the pile of 'em, and let him pick out what he wanted, seeing he was in a hurry," explained Ellen, "but he seemed to think he'd better wait till you come, so I let him. But I was bound I wouldn't wake you up, if he stayed all day!"

"Thank you, Ellen, but never fear to waken me when he—or any one—is waiting. Has he been here long?"

"No, only ten minutes or so, and he's got that album 'ts got your pictures ranged along ever sence you was a baby. I guess he'll git along. What shall I 'phone that Hapgood girl?"

"Ask her to come in an hour from now, if she can. Oh, is that my new house-gown? You have it all finished, and how pretty it is! Had I better put it on?"

"That's what 'twas made for, wa'n't it? Of course!"

Ellen, herself, adjusted its lace and ribbons, then watched Joyce's descent to the lower floor with approving eyes.

"There ain't many 'twould make her look so well on so little, that's certain. But then again there ain't many that needs so little to make 'em look well, so I guess it's a stand-off. And she's always pleased with what I do, and that's comforting," she remarked to the balustrade.

George Dalton stepped forward to meet his employer with extended hand, and did not immediately resign the fingers committed to his clasp.

"I felt that I nearly walked you to death yesterday," he observed apologetically, "and ought to assure myself of your health this morning. You look very fresh and beau—and ready for anything."

"Oh, I am; though I was up half the night in addition, which explains my laziness this morning. I suppose you know who has come?"

"No, I've not heard. Mr. Barrington hasn't ventured into the wilds, has he? Or that other lawyer, Mr. West?"

"No." Joyce shook her head, shrinking unaccountably from making the simple statement, and wishing Ellen had been more communicative with the visitor. "It's Madame Bonnivel's son, the naval officer, Leon."

"Oh!"

The little exclamation was prolonged, and something seemed to die out of the young man's face. To her own disgusted surprise she felt herself trembling and flushing. How silly it all was! The manager stepped back stiffly, and picked up his soft hat from the chair upon which he had carelessly tossed it when he came bravely in, a few moments since, feeling himself an assured and welcome guest. As he regained it the old, stern manner, almost forgotten of late, fell over him like a mantle.

"This Bonnivel has been in the war, has he?"

"No, not in active service. They have been kept cruising between Florida and Key West, on guard duty. His ship is the 'Terror'?"

"Ah!"

He looked at her, trying to remember where that name had come up before. Then it appeared to him in a flash.

"Why, that's where Lozcoski served?"

"Yes, I suppose so."

"And you tried to question him about the captain's name."

"You see, I wanted to make sure that he was on that ship. His forgetting seemed to make it doubtful."

"But is this Bonnivel captain?"

"Oh, no indeed, only lieutenant of the engineering corps. He is quite young."

He looked at her blankly, and felt himself Methuselah in his thirty-fourth year. He could not think of another question to ask, so, fingering his hat in awkward fashion, turned slowly as if to leave, his errand quite forgotten.

Joyce felt the chill that had come over him, but could not see how to dispel it. There seemed nothing to say, though there had been a thousand things yesterday. How stupid she must seem!

"I—I'm expecting Lucy," she brought out finally, catching at this straw of a subject gladly. "I wonder what she can want to see me about so particularly."

"Did you tell her she was to be subp[oe]naed as witness for the prosecution?" he asked, trying to be business-like.

"No, I didn't. I'm afraid it will trouble her greatly."

"Doubtless." His manner dropped into listlessness, and by slow stages he now reached the door. He would have been out of it in a second when a quick tap on the other, which opened into a side corridor, was followed by the entrance of Camille, with her brother in tow.

"Are you up at last?" she cried gaily. "We've been waiting hours for you—oh, good morning, Mr. Dalton."

That gentleman bowed stiffly from the doorway, and Joyce with an effort, drew herself together.

"Good morning, Camille! Leon, this is Mr. Dalton, of whom you have heard so much in my letters. You will scarcely need to scrape acquaintance. What's on the docket this morning, Gypsy?"

Leon had advanced smilingly, with extended hand, prepared

to fully like the man who had been such an able assistant to Joyce. But the sudden consciousness that it was only as her employee that this young officer had thought of him, and Joyce's own outspoken declaration as to the correspondence between them, stung George Dalton to the quick.

He was not versed in the ways of society, and this insecurity left him helpless how to act in such an emergency. To ignore it never occurred to him; he could only resent it. He bowed too low to see Leon's extended hand, and saying frostily, "I am honored to meet you, sir!" turned on his heel and stalked out with no further word.

"The coolness of him!" cried Camille, indignantly, while her brother's dark eyes turned astonishedly from one to the other.

"Was I to blame? What ailed him anyhow?" he asked quickly.

"Just a lack of good manners," returned Camille in a disgusted tone. "One never knows where such people will break out next."

Joyce felt something flare up so hotly within her that she had to turn away, so that neither might notice her deep chagrin. She changed the subject entirely by her next remark, and Dalton's name was not again mentioned.

But when Camille proposed the drive the two had planned, Joyce found Lucy's promised call a sufficient excuse to decline going. Her neighbors would not be so easily put off, however.

"How absurd, Joyce! 'Phone her to come later, can't you? We'll be back by two or three o'clock. You know Leon's furlough only lasts a fortnight."

"But it may be a grave matter with Lucy. Have you told Leon of our tragic happenings, here? I believe I have not written them?" giving him a quick glance.

"No, you haven't—nor anything else. I began to think you had dropped me from your list, Joyce."

"I have been so busy. No, I must not put Lucy off just for my own pleasure."

"And ours." Leon was studying her face with a thoughtful expression on his own. She seemed unreal to him, somehow.

"Oh, I shall claim all the rest of your day. I want you all to come over for dinner to-night, down to Dodo. You won't disappoint me?"

"I don't know," pouted Camille, unappeased.

"Well, I do," said Leon heartily, still oblivious to currents and counter-currents. "I shall come at any rate, and I doubt not the rest will come trailing after. Perhaps, Joyce, you won't refuse a drive alone with me, to-morrow?"

"We will see."

"I know you have plenty of calls upon your time, but I won't keep you long. Will you go?"

He looked straight into her eyes with the old commanding manner, which she had never been able to resist. She smiled and murmured "Yes," but, to her own dazed surprise, her whole soul roused up to whisper emphatically "*No!*"

And she did not go, after all. When Lucy appeared it was to beg with tears that she might be taken to see poor Nate, and

Joyce gladly promised all that she desired. Her pride once broken down, Lucy sobbed and cried in an abandon of sorrow, letting her childish heart lie bare beneath Joyce's tender gaze. The latter told the child she could not leave that day on account of the dinner-party, but would be ready early in the morning for the first train.

"I will have to excuse myself to Leon," she thought with an odd lightening at her heart.

And then, as the vision of his fine face and figure, his grace of manner, his joyous frankness and charm of conversation, rose before her, a wave of astonishment, almost of protest, swept over her till the tears rose in her eyes. What had so changed her that she should be glad to avoid her old friend?

The dinner, as Camille remarked once or twice, was a strictly family affair. Mrs. Phelps, who happened in on an errand just as they were gathering, so reported it at her own tea-table, soon afterwards, with glowing comments on the "handsome young officer" who had just come home.

Her nephew listened without replying, and did not finish his second delicate muffin, though she had baked them herself with the expectation that he would dispose of several, as was his custom. She noticed, but set it down to some unknown bother over business, and wondered whether there had been trouble with any of the furnaces, or if some order had been returned on his hands. She knew too much to ask, though. It was never easy to question George, even in his most relaxed moods. Joyce was about the only one who had ever attempted it successfully.

The meal over, he wandered outside, and stood with his hands in his pockets, looking aimlessly around him, with a feeling of wonder mingled with his sense of desolation. It had never occurred to him, before, to find time hanging heavily on his hands, to wonder what he should do next. Work had always driven him, and even after his special hours were over, there were countless duties for the manager. Then, it was always such a delight to find a few moments for reading, where he had so little leisure that a lull was seized with avidity.

But to-night the very thought of bills, or books, disgusted him! He turned sharply away from the factory, and, avoiding the knoll at the other end of town, struck out for the open country. It happened to be the road Dan so often traveled, though George did not know that. He found its scenes entirely new, had he noticed them. He was not a man who found much time for country strolls.

It was not yet dark, and the pink glow of a fine sunset still lingered in the air, which was soft and still. The first frosts had tinged the outermost leaves of the maples, and the sumach was brilliant in the hedges, yet the bulk of the foliage was still green, for in that locality winter held off, sometimes, until December ushered him in. The green of the trees, vivified by the late rains, thrown out against this rosy sky, was as satisfying as the odor of flowering currant in the early spring. It made one love the world. The dust was beaten down into smooth swirls in the road, and the footpath, worn in the sod alongside, felt hard as cement under his leather soles. The silence and beauty of it all soothed him, and the rhythm of his own tramp, tramp, steadied his nerves and relieved the tension at his throat. He began to relax from jaw to instep, and presently found himself softly whistling one of the late coon songs, with its quaint "rag-time," which had caught his ear and held his memory ever since he had heard it, a week or two ago.

At a certain place the footpath broke and mingled with

others. Glancing up and around, he saw a wood at his side, and just here a cattle-gate in the rail fence, through which a herd had evidently passed, not long since, to be milked and housed in the home barn for the night. The gate was left carelessly open, as if it did not matter now, and, lured by the dark interior, he slipped in.

It took a nimble winding in and out to avoid tree-roots, underbrush, and marshy tracts, till at length he came to an open glade by a small stream. It impressed him how regularly the trees grew about this glade. They seemed trimmed up just so high, like a hedge. After a moment's thought, he discovered the reason. The trimming was done by the cattle, and the length of their stretched necks determined the height of the trimming. A gardener with clippers could not have made a neater job of it.

Pleased with the beauty of the spot, he lingered some time. Nature's charm was almost an unknown quantity to him, but it held him in close bonds to-night. After a while, as it darkened, he rose from the fallen log upon which he had been sitting, and began to follow the little stream, still wrapped in far-away thoughts. The twilight had settled into a night that was moonless, but had that luminosity often seen on clear nights in late autumn. He could see all about him, even in the wood. As he reached another somewhat open space, coming upon it silently from behind a thick growth of underbrush, with only the narrow cow-path to cut it, a sound arrested him, and, lying flat on the ground, he saw the figure of a man. The sound was a groan.

CHAPTER XXVII

NIGHT HAPPENINGS

He stopped, paralyzed into rigidity for the instant, and a sobbing voice broke upon him,

"Oh, if I could only know! Is she yours, or not? Why can't you come out of space and answer me? I would have given my heart's blood for you, yet it seems as if, all the time, I must seem to take yours. What was Rachel to you, Will? Answer! Answer!"

The cry was almost a shriek, but Dalton knew the voice, and, after the instant's dazed astonishment, comprehended the scene. His first impulse, which he would have acted upon a few weeks since, was to steal away undetected; his second, born of his own sadness to-night, was to stay and help the poor fellow, if he could. He took a step forward, and spoke softly,

"Dan!"

The boy sat up with a sudden jerk, and gazed at him, wide-eyed, white as the froth in the stream's eddies.

"Will!" he whispered. "Have you come at last?"

"No, no, Dan! It's I, Dalton. I just happened here, or possibly I was sent. How do we know, but Will directed me here? My poor boy, let me sit beside you and tell you something. May I?"

Dan bowed his head respectfully, as he muttered,

"Oh, the boss!"

"Listen, Dan. I know how this tragic death of your brother's has preyed upon you. and cut you off from your friends. But can't you see, in the light of poor Nate's similar experience, how little you are blamed—how, instead, you are sympathized with? Have you heard a word from the boys, except pity for him? It was a terrible accident in both cases, and worse in yours, but neither you nor Nate can be blamed."

"But they've got him shut up."

"Until the matter can be tried, yes. I haven't a doubt of his acquittal, though, and it's better for Nate to be tried and acquitted, than to have the affair left in doubt."

"I almost wish they'd tried me."

"Why, Dan, there was never even a charge against you. Everybody, from the coroner out, knew it was an accident. And Dan, I'm going to say one thing more. Your brother was not engaged to Rachel Hemphill. I *know* that!"

Dan started.

"How?" he whispered huskily.

"From his own lips. It was only a few days before he—went. I came upon them talking together, and Will, saying good-by to her, turned and joined me, to ask some question, or other.

I liked him well, as you know, and began guying him a little about Rachel; and what do you think he said?"

"What?"

"He laughed out in his happy way, and looked me in the face with dancing eyes. 'Why, don't you know—but of course you don't,' he said, 'for I found it all out by accident, myself. Rache isn't the girl to give herself away, and you mustn't let on if I tell you.' I promised good faith and he bent over and said, low and gently, 'I'm awfully fond of Rache, but not that way. It's for a sister I want her, and perhaps I'll have her, too. For I've found out she's gone on Dan—dear old Dan! Isn't that too good to be true?' And then he actually squeezed my hand in his joy."

Dan had clutched at Dalton's knee, as if to steady himself, and sat strained forward, his whole being concentrated in the act of listening. At length he slowly turned his head, and gazed steadily into the other's eyes. A star, just above the little opening where they sat, lighted them with its shining. Each could see to read the truth in the other's face.

"You are speaking as before God, George Dalton?"

"As before God, Daniel Price."

"Then may He bless you forever!"

Their hands clasped warmly and, after a little while, during which neither had spoken, Dan stood up.

"I want to go home and think about it," he said.

"And, first, I'm going to a place I have near here, to get some things. It's a place I won't need any more. I'm going to put the whole thing back of me, and live like Will did. Don't you think that will please him best?"

"I know it will, Dan."

"And Mr. Dalton, it ain't any of my business, but us folks can't help noticing how things are going with our bosses—specially when we're fond of them. I hope it's true about you and Miss Lavillotte, for I believe you're just made for each other—you don't mind my speaking out?"

"No, Dan; it's all been speaking out to-night. Just between ourselves and the Heaven up there. And, in that way, I'll say, I'm afraid, my boy, I'm afraid! She's away beyond me."

"She's a beauty, and like a queen, but she isn't too good for you, sir."

"Thank you, Dan, but you don't know all."

Dalton had risen now, and they stood facing each other. Something in his voice made Dan look at him keenly.

"Rachel has suspected something, and she's whispered it to me, sir. We've been wondering if there *is* a 'young Early,' and if there isn't—" He stopped, and Dalton's hand pressed his arm.

"Dan, I can trust you and Rachel?"

"To the death, sir!"

"Then, you understand. She is the one. She owns it all. You see, now, why I cannot aspire to her."

"No, sir, I don't! I see why you're just the man to help her in doing a great, good work, and making of us all the loyalest workmen that ever lived. Don't you never give her up, sir, never!"

"Not if there are older claimants on the field?"

"But are there?"

"One has come—a spruce young naval officer—no, I'll be fair;—a fine, handsome, well-bred fellow, every inch a man in appearance. And she corresponds with him."

"But what could he do in her life, sir? He'd pull one way, and she another. Don't you give her up!"

"I'll hang till she shakes me, Dan!" laughed the other, lapsing into the slang of the men as his hopes rose.

They said good-night and took their several ways, Dan to break up the little retreat in the woods, which he no longer needed, since hope and action were to supersede despair and remorseful grief; Dalton to tramp sturdily back to the village, resolved to wait and work.

As he neared the settlement he noticed lights ablaze in Bachelor's Row, and many figures flitting about with hurried movements. He stopped to inquire the cause. Mrs. Hemphill edged her way close to him, breaking in before the slower speech of the man so questioned had forced its way out.

"Why, you see Murfree's dead, at last. He's been trying to fling hisself out o' bed agin, an' it took three men to hold him. In the struggle he just cullopsed and died. They wasn't nobody but Dan could keep him down lately, and Dan's gone some'ers to-night."

She had scarcely finished when the lad, on a well-weighted wheel, sprinted into view. Dalton called him.

"This way, Dan," and he flung himself off.

"What is it? Murfree off again?"

"Yes," walking beside the boy as he led his wheel on a detour around the group. "Off forever, poor fellow! They were trying to keep him on the bed when he 'cullopsed,' they tell me."

The word had impressed Dalton, and he could not refrain from using it himself, smiling over it in the darkness. But Dan did not notice.

"I oughtn't to have left him, but I got so down-hearted I had to. Come around through my room, and we can get in without forcing this crowd. I want to put up my bike."

They were soon in the apartment which Murfree had occupied, just across from the cobbler's. Dr. Browne stood over the bed, and had the two watchers guarding the door to keep out the frankly-curious people without. They thronged up to its lintels just as the surf presses against the dykes, that are the doors of the land, to guard it from that strange old sea which would learn all its secrets, only to obliterate them. The doctor looked up. "He is resting at last," he said in brusque fashion, "and a good thing for everybody. Did you ever see this mark on him, Dan? Regular tatooing, isn't it?"

They both examined the bare shoulder, and, on its curve into the arm, observed the red and blue marking, plainly defined on the white skin. A circle formed of twisted snakes, head to head and with tails intertwined, enclosed a monogram, apparently, but the letters were not English in character, and so intermingled that none of the three could separate them.

"I've seen that, or what's just like it," said Dan hurriedly. "It's stamped on some papers he give me to keep once, when he was himself for a few minutes. He said, if he died I might open 'em, and they'd secure justice. He didn't say justice to who. Then he went off again, mumbling and muttering. I never could find out just what he wanted me to do with 'em."

"We'll look into that," said Dalton, who had his own ideas concerning the dead man. "We can't do any more here, doctor?"

"No. I'll turn him over to these boys, now. They know what to do; and I've got to go back to Jim Dodge's to-night. His little girl's down with measles—severe case."

Dalton busied himself for a few moments with Murfree's effects, then, beckoning Dan, they went back into the lad's room at the rear.

"I wish you'd let me see those papers," said Dalton, in his authoritative voice, and soon the two were pouring over a small book, written full; a document or two on parchment; a badge, in which the letters and the twisted serpents were wrought out of gun-metal into a cheap-looking pin; and several letters. Neither said much as they passed these from hand to hand, Dalton fully recognizing the right of his workman to know the full contents of what had been left in his care; the other never questioning the manager's interest and concern in all matters pertaining to his employees. As Dalton rose to go, he said:

"My boy, you fully understand the importance of keeping this to yourself, till we need it in evidence?"

Fannie E. Newberry

"Yes, sir; I do."

"Well, I know you are to be trusted. Put them in some safe place, under lock and key, and wait till I give you the word. Good-night."

He went out the back way, though the crowd was mostly dispersed now, and, as he gained the street, glanced over toward the park. At its other end a light still gleamed in an upper window of the pretty house, and he hoped it was Joyce's window, for he was in that romantic stage, never fully explained by the psychologists, where every inanimate thing becomes interesting just in proportion to the nearness of its connection with one person—oftentimes a very ordinary young person to outsiders.

It was decidedly out of his way, but he plunged into the park shadows, and hastened through it, then stood in the narrow street which separated its broad end from Joyce's confines, and gazed up at the light.

His devotion ought to have been rewarded—perhaps it was.

Presently the glow fell off into a glimmer, but, as he was turning away, another sprang into brightness below. This he knew to be the library, and it gave him an idea which he was quick to act upon. He took a sprinter's pace for home, and, as soon as he arrived there, made straight for the telephone, where he called up Miss Lavillotte. In a moment her gentle "Hello!" came softly to his ears, and his face took on the look of a satisfied idiot, or possibly an inspired poet seeking for a rhyme; the eyes upturned and the mouth open.

"Do you know who is talking?" he asked.

"Yes; Mr. Dalton."

"You are right!" as if she had mastered an intricate problem. "And I would not have disturbed you, but I have great news for you."

"Indeed?"

"Yes. Murfree died an hour or two ago, and has left papers that tell the whole story, and exonerate Lozcoski."

"How glad I am!"

"I knew you would be. There are other things, too. When can I see you?"

"Let me see. I have news, too. Lucy has broken down at last, and begged me, all tears and softness, to take her to see poor Nate. We are going in the morning at 8.15. But that would be too early for you?"

"Not at all. And you and Lucy can't go alone to the jail. If you will allow me—"

"How if I command you?" merrily.

"Then I can do nothing but obey."

"Well, then, I do. We'll take the same train, won't we—that 8.15?"

"Yes, of course."

"Good-night, then."

"Good-night—till morning."

He distinguished a funny little sound, like a suppressed

giggle, and in a clear, final tone came a last "Good-night, my friend!"

Then he heard her receiver click in its socket, and the decided tinkle of the bell shut him off. But he did not care. He was still her "friend." He would be with her all to-morrow. His interests and hers were identical, and nobody should interfere without a struggle on his part.

Not that he meant anything overt, or aggressive. Only he would make himself so necessary she could not do without him.

CHAPTER XXVIII

VISITING THE SHUT-INS

Poor Nate fretted in confinement, but not for his own sake. He simply ignored his surroundings, not deigning to complain, or scarcely to notice; but sought every opportunity to ask eagerly after the welfare of Lucy and her little family. He overwhelmed Mr. Barrington with questions, somewhat to the bewilderment of the old gentleman, who could not distinctly grasp the idea that Nate was self-constituted protector in place of the man he was accused of murdering.

He flung his eager queries at Mr. Dalton, and more gently pelted Joyce; and the one or two "boys," who had been admitted to his cell, departed with the dazed consciousness that, instead of finding out "all about it" from Nate, as had been their intention, he had kept them busy telling insignificant home events, until they were pumped dry of every drop of knowledge they possessed.

But when the door opened that gray morning, and a little figure swathed in black came slowly in, Nate scarcely moved. He sat still on his bunk, staring at her till she threw back the long veil, and said reproachfully,

"Nate!"

Fannie E. Newberry

"Is it really you, Lucy?" he asked, slowly rising and making a step forward. "I never see you like this. I most thought 'twas your ghost. Set down, child. 'Tain't much of a place, but—" He drew out the one chair they allowed him in the narrow cell, and, as he placed it, Lucy caught his rough hand between her own.

"Nate, aren't you glad to see me?" she cried, fresh tears springing to her already overtaxed eyes.

He looked down at her, nodded gravely, and then laughed a little.

"Why, in course I'm glad, Lucy! You know that without tellin', don't ye? I ain't much on talkin', Lucy, but you know me."

Lucy stayed as long as they would let her, while Joyce and George sat on a stone bench in the corridor. The visit seemed short to them, but the turnkey was impatient long before the half-hour was up, feeling himself *de trop* all around. After the strangeness wore off, something of the old natural friendliness came back into Nate's manner, and Lucy's tears ceased to flow, as her tongue wagged ever more cheerfully.

They talked entirely about the little home-doings—Tilly's streak of facility in washing dishes without breakage; Rufie's month's record in school; the big baby's latest attempt at the English vocabulary; and the little baby's first tooth. Lucy told, too, of Joyce's kindness and constant oversight, and of Dalton's promise that her father's pay should not be stopped this quarter at least. Scarcely a word of the tragedy between them, or of the trial before Nate.

Just as she was leaving, however, she said timidly, "Shall I come in to it, Nate—the trial, you know?"

"Guess likely you'll have to, my girl. You'll be a witness, you see."

"Oh, will I, Nate? And for you? I'll try to help you all I can!"

"Well, no! I guess it's t'other side'll call you, Lucy. But don't you mind. Just tell the truth and shame the devil! Them lawyers is a tricky pack, and they know how to mix a fellow up, till he don't know crystal from frit. But don't you worrit! The truth's stronger'n the whole pack of 'em, and that's what I'm a-restin' on. You tell the truth as you b'lieve it, whether it's for me or agin' me, child, and it's all I'll ask o' you."

"Nate, I saw you didn't try to hit pa when you had the stick and was right over him, but you'll own up you was awful mad?"

"Yes, I was: and for the first minute I was murderin' mad, 'count o' you. I'll own that. But, you seen when I got it under me and was leadin' him off peaceable, didn't you? I slipp'd back'ard and flung up my arms, and then the thing struck wrong. You couldn't think I meant that blow, Lucy?"

"No, I know you didn't. I see it all, now. I was so scared then I couldn't think, but—"

"Time's up, miss," said the officer resolutely, and Lucy hurried out, scarcely waiting to shake hands while the others merely gave Nate a smile and word through the barred door.

They knew from his face it was all he needed to-day.

*   *   *   *   *

When Leon heard about the Pole who had shipped for a short time on the "Terror," he listened to the talk of him with interest, and asked permission to accompany Joyce and her manager at their next interview. By the time the four (for Camille was of the party, too) made their call at the jail, the faces of the two more frequent visitors were pretty well known there. Lozcoski, now well fed, and filled with hope and comfort, through the communications of the interpreter, was not the same man who had burst his way into the Social-house a few weeks ago. His staring eyes had softened, his hollow cheeks rounded out, his prison-cut hair could not mat now, and through his clean-shaven lips white teeth gleamed smilingly at times. The wolf had vanished, and the man was now installed in the body that needed only refinement and thought to make it comely.

The minute Leon entered, alone, leaving the rest outside, he rose quickly and gave the naval salute—the inside of the hand to the temple held palm forward—of a U. S. man-of-war's-man to his superior officer. He had recognized the young lieutenant at once. This pleased Leon Bonnivel, and he entered into brisk conversation with him, through the interpreter, soon becoming convinced that the man told the truth about his service and its ending. Thus the chain of evidence which was to free an honest, but unfortunate man, grew link by link, and Joyce formed the clasp which held all together.

She was allowed to enter after awhile, and the Pole's face lighted almost into rapture at sight of her. He knew what she had done for him, and he felt that no ikon of his hut in the old country had ever seemed more beautiful, or more worthy of his honor. He would have knelt to her readily enough, but that his few months in America had taught him that such demonstrations were not admissible on democratic soil. So he merely stood in awkward adoration, and beamed upon her.

She spoke a few kind words, telling him his discharge papers would soon be ready and that he was then to report for work in Littleton, if he so desired, and was turning away when, after a quickly-spoken sentence by Lozcoski, the interpreter said explanatorily,

"He bids me thank you, lady, and give you the blessing of a man at peace with his God. And he asks, where is your young husband that he may thank him, also."

"My husband!" stammered Joyce, while Leon turned sharply to gaze at her flushing cheeks. "Wh—what does he mean? I have no husband."

The interpreter, trying to control his smiles, explained, and the Pole, after a disconcerted expression had crossed his face, smiled blandly also and, spreading out both hands, spoke again.

"He begs the lady's pardon," said the interpreter. "It was her betrothed that he meant. The young man who is boss at the Works. He thought you were married, rather than betrothed, ma'am. But he is glad to ask blessings on your future union."

What could Joyce say? To keep on explaining and protesting would be ridiculous, and it suddenly flashed across her mind that the mistake was natural. As this Lozcoski had seen them together in close companionship, and intimate counsel, he had a right to believe what he did. Such personal business relations, without marriage or betrothal, nearly as sacred and irrevocable, would be an impossibility between two of their age and social standing in his own country.

So she simply bowed her head, accepted the murmured blessings of the grateful prisoner, and hurried out, leaving the animated lexicon she had hired—all one broad smile of intelligence now—to interpret her actions as best he could.

Fannie E. Newberry

CHAPTER XXIX

A DREAM ENDED

Joyce could only hope nothing had been heard in the corridor, but her first surreptitious glance was not consolatory. Camille, with an expression oddly commingled of mirth and petulance, was intensely busy with her glove-fastening, while the broad back of George Dalton, who was apparently as busy gazing from a barred window against a stone wall, had a most uncanny look of intelligence about it. As for the sheriff—he did not try to conceal the grin with which he looked at that back, and then at Joyce, who would have given a large slice of her fortune for a sheltering veil to cover her face, just then. As the party marched out into the open air there was an appearance of constraint about them. Camille kept persistently at her brother's side, and Joyce was forced to follow with George. He tried so hard to look noncommittal that he only succeeded in looking thoroughly cross, and Leon was shut within himself, evidently dazed, but trying to think the thing out.

The tension did not loosen as they made their way to the great depot, just in time to board the earlier of the "dinner trains," at 5.13. But, as they passed in, Joyce circumvented any further such pairing off by calmly seating herself by Camille, and leaving the young men to adjust themselves as they would.

Few realize the many disagreeable trifles that accompany the movements of any notable personage. Joyce was often pointed out as the great heiress, who had eschewed city society to manage her business affairs in person, and Leon's air, even in civilian dress, was observable. Many eyes were turned upon the little party, who were presently seated near together in the train, and Joyce broke the spell of rigidity by leaning over to Leon and remarking, *sotto voce*,

"If you had only worn your uniform everybody would have stared. Now I think there are as many as three who have not noticed us. Is there no way of stirring up those three?"

His ready laughter answered her sally, and the strain was relieved.

But when they reached the home station Dalton proved that he was not lacking in tact, at least. Carelessly assuming that Joyce was thoroughly well escorted, he bade the trio a cheerful good-night on the platform, and struck off for his own home, without even a backward glance.

Leon nodded approvingly, all to himself.

"The fellow has self-control, anyhow," he thought, as he offered an arm to Joyce and laughingly bade Camille follow in their wake, like a good child—for the walks were narrow.

Arrived at the knoll, Joyce would not accept their invitation in to dinner, declaring she dare not so disappoint her own cook, who would be awaiting her. Neither would the brother and sister accept of her counter-invitation, saying that they had more than a cook to disappoint; namely, their mother, So they went their separate ways, but lights streamed across from window to window, like cables of trust and friendship.

It had not been an easy thing for Leon to see his mother alone in a household which made her its center and circumference, but that evening, when she retired to her room, he followed close upon her steps.

"Mayn't I come in, mother?" he asked, after tapping lightly. "I want an old-fashioned good-night talk."

She welcomed him eagerly.

"Find the best chair, dear, and draw it up by me, here. I do so enjoy this little grate on cool nights! I can feel the warmth, and imagine the light, while it all fills me with comfort and peace."

"In a minute, mother. Let me tramp about a little, first. I like to try my sea-legs on a stretch of thick carpet, occasionally. Besides, I want to look around. How snug and handsome you are here! That toilet-table is really sumptuous, and these fine etchings show off well against that soft flesh tint on the walls. Mother, you have found a good son in Larry!"

"A dear, good son, Leon. But his means are not so large as his heart. This room is mostly Joyce's gift, you know. When she gave the house she insisted on personally superintending the fittings of this room. I told her it was useless to waste beauty on me, but she said no surroundings could quite suit me, except a certain kind, and she claimed to understand that style better than any one else. She is doing for us all the time."

"She could not be other than generous—but how she has changed, mother!"

"Changed! Do you think so?"

"How could I help thinking so? I left her a shrinking, clinging child. I find her a self-poised, queenly woman. Do you remember how I used to plan to protect and defend her? I was to earn money for her and you, and to ward off all trouble from you both. It was my youthful inspiration. I return to find she needs neither money, position, protection, nor devotion. She has all, and more, than she desires. A defender would be an absurdity! All she can require now is a—manager."

His mother turned about in her chair with a distressed look.

"Leon, your tone is not bitter, but your words are."

"No, indeed! I am merely stating facts. To be bitter would be foolish. But I see it all, mother."

"Oh, Leon, it breaks my heart!"

"I feared it would, and that is why I want to talk with you." He came closer and drew up a chair. She caught his hand and held it in a close clasp. "The strange thing is, it does not break my heart at all."

He brought out each word with deliberate emphasis. Madame Bonnivel felt her blindness then as never in her life before. Oh, to be able to search his eyes, to look down into his very soul! Would he deliberately deceive his mother, to save her pain? Yet the touch of his hand was cool and calm.

"I thought you loved my Joyce!" she cried sharply, her nerves at a tension.

"I do. I always have. I always shall. And I admire her in

addition, now. She is a noble, remarkable girl. But she is a duchess, a queen, and she is as absorbed in her little kingdom as any German countess in her petty domain. Its ways and doings are of supreme importance to her, and other things do not count. It is right enough she should feel so, and she will lead a useful life. But how could it ever accord with mine? She is Lady Bountiful, and rules through love and wisdom. I am officer on a man-of-war, and command with sternness and inflexibility, never bending to coaxing or cajolery. Her ambition is to serve and uplift; mine to hold down with a steady hand, that my men may do my bidding like intelligent machines. We both may do good in our spheres, but we would inevitably pull apart, if we tried to unite them. Could I take the place of prime minister to my lady, and content myself with carrying out her orders, and expending her money? I would die first!" He sprang up and began walking about again, his voice deepening as he progressed with his subject. "Imagine me examining her books at the works, or pottering about on errands of mercy among her glass-blowers! I, who can daily tread the magnificent decks of the 'Terror,' and lead my squad on engineering feats that stir every drop of blood in my body to pride over our glorious achievements! Dearest mother, it wouldn't do."

"But, if she loves you, she would give this all up—"

"And go with me? She couldn't, mother. You know that. There is no place for women on a war-ship."

"No, but you have furloughs occasionally. She might live here, just the same—"

"With Dalton for her manager? No, thank you, mother! I am not such an idiot as that."

"But Leon! Leon! It has been my dream for years."

"And, like most dreams, is but a dissolving view. Let us hope this dream may dissolve into a scene of deeper reality, which shall far exceed the vision. You are safely anchored here beside her, and in all love and fealty she is, and will be, your daughter. I shall always feel safe and happy to know she is beside you. But the currents of my life run in broader channels. The tide floats me far out into stirring, trying scenes. I should mope myself to death here. I should hate and despise my inaction!"

"Leon, how your voice thrills! You love your work?"

"I never knew how much till now. I tell you, frankly, I returned expecting to marry Joyce, if she would have me. I am glad to understand that she most assuredly would not. I cannot tell you how suffocatingly small seems the life of a private citizen of small means on shore. My pay is little enough, we know, and I can never expect anything beyond a fair living. But what is that to me? I am backed by a government that gives me assurance, standing, power, wherever I may be. I have for friends and associates the brave and honorable, the world over. I am as proud of my ship as other men of beautiful estates, and as fond of my brave men as others of their children. I do love Joyce, even as I willingly relinquish her, but I know even she could not make up to me for all I would give up in marrying her, and resigning my commission. I see it as plainly as if inspired. Our ways must lie apart!"

"Leon, I see arguments are useless, and I will not plead for Joyce, even with my own son."

"The pleading would have to be on the other side, dearest. Remember, she does not love me."

"She did, and she would, but for this fortune and this work!

Her father always came between us in life; his accursed money must separate us now—go, Leon! My soul is bitter within me. I shall be unjust and wicked, if I say one word more."

He went slowly, reluctantly, looking back at her pale, drawn face in an anguish of pity. He knew that, brave as he had been, he had not made her wound the less. The dream of her life was ended.

CHAPTER XXX

A RAILROAD WEDDING

There was a sudden outbreak of wild enthusiasm as the verdict was given, quickly checked by the court's gavel, then all craned their necks while in a few kind words, the judge congratulated and dismissed the prisoner. Then counsel and friends gathered about Nate with outstretched hands, till his arm ached with the constant pumping, and his tongue was tied with the excitement and confusion. To steady himself he kept his eyes mostly on a little black figure, some distance away. It was close by the side of Miss Lavillotte, but its face never turned from watching him; and he knew that, from the hour the young girl had stood bravely in court and exonerated him from all blame, she had put the sad past behind her and accepted a brighter, happier future. He was only longing, now, to reach her side, but even with Dalton's efforts it was almost impossible to make their way through the press. Somehow, Nate's friends seemed to spring up from everywhere, to-day. Each official, from jailer to judge, had learned to like him, the newspaper men were his staunch allies, and the jurors had a fellow-feeling for him.

He had clung to the clean, unvarnished truth in dogged fashion, and had so impressed all by his simple story, in which he seemed only trying to tell facts, no matter how they

Fannie E. Newberry

bore upon himself, that even the prosecutor was out of conceit with his side of the case.

So the gratulatory crowd gathered thickly about him, and the little group of home-friends had to wait long before he could reach them, near the private door by the clerk's desk.

Lucy, trembling all over, caught his hand as soon as she could reach it, and fairly pulled him from the court-room. "Let's get out of this!" she whispered excitedly. "I can't breathe here. Oh, Nate, to think you are safe and it's all over. Thank God! Thank God!"

"Come," said Dalton to Joyce, who stood hesitantly, not sure there was no more to attend to, "the carriage is below and we've just time to make our train. We can say all our says in there."

He took Joyce's arm with an odd mixture of tenderness, deference, and authority, while the others followed their rapid pace. Once inside the closed vehicle, Nate seemed less excited than any of them, speaking in the same slow, even tones he always used. When Lucy, clinging to his hand, would break out, "Oh, isn't it good—isn't it too good, Nate?" he would only smile and look down at her with a tender,

"Why, yes, Lucy, it's good, but not too good, as I see. It's right, that's all. I didn't need shutting up, and I'm glad I didn't get sentenced that way. 'Twould 'a' come tough on you and the youngsters."

"I expect there'll be something of a demonstration, Nate," said the manager. "I had West 'phone the verdict to Littleton, and tell the boys to lay off the rest of the day. They'll be crazy, I presume! I know you don't care for such things, but you'll have to put up with being a hero just this once."

"Hope they won't do nothin' rash 'round them railroad tracks," said Nate, a bit anxiously. "The boys sometimes forgits theirselves when they gets to celebratin'. They don't mean nothin', but they forgits. Who'd you leave the babbies with, Lucy?"

"They're all going to be in school till three, for the teacher said Rufie might bring even the little baby to the kindergarten. Then Marry's out of the office, and she'll keep 'em till we get there at half-past four. She won't let nothing happen."

"Well, I'd 'a' been satisfied just to go home and set down and eat my supper, but never mind," sighed Nate in wistful fashion. "Folks is cur'ous about such things. Just because a man don't git sent up for what he didn't do can't make a hero outen him, as I see. But it's nice of you all to care." He looked at Joyce, sitting opposite with Dalton, he and Lucy having been given the back seat together, and a smile played about his lips and eyes, crinkling the kindly muscles into radiating lines of sunshine. "I've had lots o' thoughts, Miss Lav'lotte, since I've been shut up, and I guess I've worked out something. It's a master place for workin' out things in your mind—a jail is."

"Is it, Nate? And what have you worked out, now?"

"Well, just this. First, it did seem queer that a handsome young lady just livin' on in our town, and no blood relation to nobody, should take such an int'rust in Lucy and me, to say nothin' of other folks. Ev'ry time 't you'd come, or send other folks to me, I kept askin' inside o' me, 'Now, what does that mean? What is it to her, anyhow?' Then, kinder sudden like, it come to me once that ev'ry single one o' the good things what's been the makin' o' Littleton begun to come along just about when you fetched up there. And when I'd figured on that a while, and remembered how you and the boss here was allays consultin' together, and how you seemed to feel jest 's if you'd got stock in us, somehow, it come to me all of a heap."

"What came to you?" asked Joyce, her brilliant eyes flashing a laughing glance towards her seat-mate.

"Why, that they mightn't be any young Early after all, and that 'twas jest possible—mind, I don't say as I've got all the twists and turns of it—but that you might, somehow or other, stand fer him. You couldn't *be* him, bein' a girl, of course, but stand fer him. Don't they have proxers, or sponsors, or some such things in law, Mr. Dalton?"

That gentleman laughed heartily, and Joyce joined in with a merry peal. Even Lucy and Nate helped the chorus, though somewhat perfunctorily, not knowing just what they were laughing at.

"How is it, Miss Lavillotte, are you standing sponsor for any one?" queried Dalton, as soon as he could get his voice.

"I hope not!" she laughed in return.

"Well," put in Nate, looking from one to the other, "it seems funny to you, I see; but if I ain't much mistooken I've heered the boss, here, talk about young Early more'n once. So they must be something to it, of course."

"There!" said Joyce. "You are convicted, Mr. Dalton. Can you set yourself right?"

"I can, if I may."

"Well, do by all means, then."

"Well, Nate, I began by first being deceived myself; then, being fairly launched in deception, I went on cheating others. There never was a young Early! No man is living by that name, that we know."

Nate looked dazed, and Lucy craned forward anxiously. "Who does own the Works, then?" she cried. "Can't we go on living in our pretty houses, and having the nice new ways? Who built the school, and the church, and the Social-house?"

"Do you like the new, so much better than the old, way, Lucy? You have had great sorrows since these changes, child."

Joyce leaned forward to the girl, kindly.

"I know, but if it had come before! How dreadful hungry and wretched we'd have been! And how would it have gone with Nate? Do you s'pose they'd ever 'a' cleared him, if they hadn't knowed he had rich friends? Oh, I can't bear to think of it before! It's like the diff'runce between being out in the cold and wet, with nobody to care, and being inside by the fire, with ev'rybody good-natured. It's easier with the work, and with the children, and with ev'rybody. There's lots of times, now, when I couldn't help singin', only I'm ashamed to. And 'tisn't me only, but Marry, and Rache, and the youngsters, and all. It's like summer, come to stay."

"Dear Lucy!" said Joyce. "You put it very pleasantly, I'm sure. But here we are at the station—explanations later!" and the bustle of making a train just about to start drew their attention elsewhere.

Once within it, they could not find seats together, and perhaps neither couple was disturbed because thus separated. George Dalton bent towards Joyce, and said:

"So you are going to give it all away?"

"No, George, I expect you to do that. Just tell them plainly and simply who I am, and what are our plans for the future. It is better not to keep it longer when the—it—is so near."

"How you shy at the word, Joyce! There are two or three with the same meaning to select from, you know—wedding, nup—"

"Sh-h! George. Some one will hear you."

"And suppose they do. Are you ashamed of it? I am not. I can't even hear one of those words without a thrill of happiness. And it isn't all for ourselves, either, dearest. There is a great work before us, and many are interested. To spend our lives together, doing for those who have been my friends ever since I was a poor, hard-working, lonely little fellow— Ah! Joyce, it is a pleasant outlook!"

He turned to the window with softened eyes, and Joyce, through some strange entangling of the thought threads, suddenly remembered her last interview with Leon before he returned to the "Terror," nearly a month ago. His ardent, dominant nature had struck her as never before, while he talked glowingly of his life, his work, his ambitions. "He will make a magnificent man!" she had thought then. "Brave, resolute, a born ruler of men. But there is one idea he has not caught, by which my life is now controlled—that the one who really ministers must have something of the servant in his make-up. We 'stoop to conquer' in humanitarianism, as well as in other love. And Leon could not stoop. We are both masterful in a way, but his mastery would overpower mine, and crush it out. I could not be free to live as I have chosen, if he had any control over me, and yet, strangely enough, I once believed I owed all my ideas of helpfulness to him. I know, now, it was the dear mother who informed my mind, while Leon controlled my fancy."

She was lost in her musings as the train shrieked out its on-coming call to the little one-room station-house, at Littleton. From the window they could see that the whole town seemed to be gathered about its doors. The platform, tracks, and surrounding buildings were black with people. As the brakes were put on, lessening their speed and the roar of the train, cheer after cheer reached them from without. The air was full of waving caps, handkerchiefs, and aprons. Now they could begin to distinguish separate groups and faces. Mrs. Hemphill, in the midst of her little brood, shook the gingham skirts of the baby in her arms, and old Mother Flaherty waggled her wide Irish border and waved her cane, in utter abandon. Dan and Rachel, standing together, looked fairly radiant; even Marie was there on her tricycle, with Babette and Gus keeping guard over her, while Lucy's children, crowding near, were shouting themselves hoarse. Every one was on hand. Close by, the cobbler, having somewhere picked up a shoe to mend, waved it frantically by its leather string. Joyce's own carriage, with Gilbert proudly controlling the restive horses, was drawn up beside the platform, and on its seat, reckless of danger, stood Camille waving the dust-cloth in utter forgetfulness of what she had in her hand. In close proximity stood Dorette, and by Dr. Browne's side, in his shambling old buggy, sat Madame Bonnivel, directing the demonstrations of Dodo, on her lap. Nate looked at Lucy an instant.

"Say, child," he said in a hesitant tone, "it's a shame to think I'm nobody but just Nate, when they've made such a fuss! Be we goin' to git married, or ain't we? I s'pose we ought to, if I'm goin' to look after you and the babbies, and it seems as if 'twould sorter pay 'em for their trouble if we'd let 'em know it, or something. Folks allays likes to hear about weddin's.

Fannie E. Newberry

Say, why don't we just go along and git married right now? Might as well, and then they'd sure be satisfied. I see the preacher a-standin' there, clost to thet ole maid of Miss Lav'lotte's, and if you say so—"

"But, Nate, I ain't dressed up! That is, not bridy, you know."

He looked down at her—such a mite in her black swathings!—and smiled.

"You ain't nothin' but a child, Lucy, and I'll have to be husband and father, both. But I'll look after you close, dear, and be good to the babbies. Come, I guess we'd better. Your clo'es is all right."

Waves of cheers greeted Nate as he stepped outside, with Lucy in tow. The crowd surged forward toward the platform, but he waved them back.

"Hello, boys!" he cried, raising his voice. "This is nice of you, but jest hold up a minute, please. We're goin' to have a weddin'—Lucy and me—'fore we all go home. Come, Lucy!"

He caught her hand in a firmer grip, and struggled toward the minister, his countenance strong in its intensity of purpose. Lucy's blossom face, that had been growing rounder and rosier every day, shone out like a vision of hope against the long black veil, which streamed behind her like a background of cloud floating away into the past. The crowd, eagerly watching, was silent with astonishment, and the young divinity student, taken thus unaware, looked really pale under his excitement. But he was a man of strong calibre and spirituality, with quickened sympathies, and that insight into human nature which some people name magnetism. He knew Lucy's story and Nate's. He felt this marriage was, under all the circumstances, right and best. Baring his head reverently, he stepped forward and raised his right hand. A solemn hush fell upon all. After a short invocation, which steadied his own nerves, and attuned all to the solemnity of the occasion, he put the momentous questions in his most impressive manner, and Nate and Lucy made their vows, the whole population of Littleton serving as witnesses. The instant the blessing was pronounced upon the wedded pair, Nate spoke up in a firm, loud voice—

"Now, friends, let's all go home and git our suppers. If you're so tired as I be you'll need 'em. Come, Lucy, the babbies are fretting, and there's Tilly tryin' to git to us. Come on!"

The crowd, laughing and crying, parted to let them through, Joyce and George, still quite dazed, staring with the rest. Camille's voice aroused them.

"Did you ever see anything so matter-of-fact! How he did take the wind out of our sails! Well, let's go home, as he says. Dr. Browne has run off with mother, but she wants you both—George and Joyce—to come home with me to dinner."

"Wait!" cried Joyce, suddenly finding her tongue. She beckoned to Dalton, spoke a hurried word or two, and in a trice Nate, Lucy, and the Hapgood children, down to the little baby, were packed into the carriage, and Gilbert bidden to drive them home for the wedding journey.

Then she waved them adieu, and turned to her friend and betrothed—

"Come, Camille; come, George, we three can walk!"

Fannie E. Newberry

Choose from Thousands of 1stWorldLibrary Classics By

A. M. Barnard
Ada Leverson
Adolphus William Ward
Aesop
Agatha Christie
Alexander Aaronsohn
Alexander Kielland
Alexandre Dumas
Alfred Gatty
Alfred Ollivant
Alice Duer Miller
Alice Turner Curtis
Alice Dunbar
Allen Chapman
Alleyne Ireland
Ambrose Bierce
Amelia E. Barr
Amory H. Bradford
Andrew Lang
Andrew McFarland Davis
Andy Adams
Angela Brazil
Anna Alice Chapin
Anna Sewell
Annie Besant
Annie Hamilton Donnell
Annie Payson Call
Annie Roe Carr
Annonaymous
Anton Chekhov
Archibald Lee Fletcher
Arnold Bennett
Arthur C. Benson
Arthur Conan Doyle
Arthur M. Winfield
Arthur Ransome
Arthur Schnitzler
Arthur Train
Atticus
B.H. Baden-Powell
B. M. Bower
B. C. Chatterjee
Baroness Emmuska Orczy
Baroness Orczy
Basil King
Bayard Taylor
Ben Macomber
Bertha Muzzy Bower
Bjornstjerne Bjornson

Booth Tarkington
Boyd Cable
Bram Stoker
C. Collodi
C. E. Orr
C. M. Ingleby
Carolyn Wells
Catherine Parr Traill
Charles A. Eastman
Charles Amory Beach
Charles Dickens
Charles Dudley Warner
Charles Farrar Browne
Charles Ives
Charles Kingsley
Charles Klein
Charles Hanson Towne
Charles Lathrop Pack
Charles Romyn Dake
Charles Whibley
Charles Willing Beale
Charlotte M. Braeme
Charlotte M. Yonge
Charlotte Perkins Stetson
Clair W. Hayes
Clarence Day Jr.
Clarence E. Mulford
Clemence Housman
Confucius
Coningsby Dawson
Cornelis DeWitt Wilcox
Cyril Burleigh
D. H. Lawrence
Daniel Defoe
David Garnett
Dinah Craik
Don Carlos Janes
Donald Keyhoe
Dorothy Kilner
Dougan Clark
Douglas Fairbanks
E. Nesbit
E. P. Roe
E. Phillips Oppenheim
E. S. Brooks
Earl Barnes
Edgar Rice Burroughs
Edith Van Dyne
Edith Wharton

Edward Everett Hale
Edward J. O'Biren
Edward S. Ellis
Edwin L. Arnold
Eleanor Atkins
Eleanor Hallowell Abbott
Eliot Gregory
Elizabeth Gaskell
Elizabeth McCracken
Elizabeth Von Arnim
Ellem Key
Emerson Hough
Emilie F. Carlen
Emily Bronte
Emily Dickinson
Enid Bagnold
Enilor Macartney Lane
Erasmus W. Jones
Ernie Howard Pie
Ethel May Dell
Ethel Turner
Ethel Watts Mumford
Eugene Sue
Eugenie Foa
Eugene Wood
Eustace Hale Ball
Evelyn Everett-green
Everard Cotes
F. H. Cheley
F. J. Cross
F. Marion Crawford
Fannie E. Newberry
Federick Austin Ogg
Ferdinand Ossendowski
Fergus Hume
Florence A. Kilpatrick
Fremont B. Deering
Francis Bacon
Francis Darwin
Frances Hodgson Burnett
Frances Parkinson Keyes
Frank Gee Patchin
Frank Harris
Frank Jewett Mather
Frank L. Packard
Frank V. Webster
Frederic Stewart Isham
Frederick Trevor Hill
Frederick Winslow Taylor

Friedrich Kerst
Friedrich Nietzsche
Fyodor Dostoyevsky
G.A. Henty
G.K. Chesterton
Gabrielle E. Jackson
Garrett P. Serviss
Gaston Leroux
George A. Warren
George Ade
Geroge Bernard Shaw
George Cary Eggleston
George Durston
George Ebers
George Eliot
George Gissing
George MacDonald
George Meredith
George Orwell
George Sylvester Viereck
George Tucker
George W. Cable
George Wharton James
Gertrude Atherton
Gordon Casserly
Grace E. King
Grace Gallatin
Grace Greenwood
Grant Allen
Guillermo A. Sherwell
Gulielma Zollinger
Gustav Flaubert
H. A. Cody
H. B. Irving
H.C. Bailey
H. G. Wells
H. H. Munro
H. Irving Hancock
H. R. Naylor
H. Rider Haggard
H. W. C. Davis
Haldeman Julius
Hall Caine
Hamilton Wright Mabie
Hans Christian Andersen
Harold Avery
Harold McGrath
Harriet Beecher Stowe
Harry Castlemon
Harry Coghill
Harry Houidini

Hayden Carruth
Helent Hunt Jackson
Helen Nicolay
Hendrik Conscience
Hendy David Thoreau
Henri Barbusse
Henrik Ibsen
Henry Adams
Henry Ford
Henry Frost
Henry James
Henry Jones Ford
Henry Seton Merriman
Henry W Longfellow
Herbert A. Giles
Herbert Carter
Herbert N. Casson
Herman Hesse
Hildegard G. Frey
Homer
Honore De Balzac
Horace B. Day
Horace Walpole
Horatio Alger Jr.
Howard Pyle
Howard R. Garis
Hugh Lofting
Hugh Walpole
Humphry Ward
Ian Maclaren
Inez Haynes Gillmore
Irving Bacheller
Isabel Cecilia Williams
Isabel Hornibrook
Israel Abrahams
Ivan Turgenev
J.G.Austin
J. Henri Fabre
J. M. Barrie
J. M. Walsh
J. Macdonald Oxley
J. R. Miller
J. S. Fletcher
J. S. Knowles
J. Storer Clouston
J. W. Duffield
Jack London
Jacob Abbott
James Allen
James Andrews
James Baldwin

James Branch Cabell
James DeMille
James Joyce
James Lane Allen
James Lane Allen
James Oliver Curwood
James Oppenheim
James Otis
James R. Driscoll
Jane Abbott
Jane Austen
Jane L. Stewart
Janet Aldridge
Jens Peter Jacobsen
Jerome K. Jerome
Jessie Graham Flower
John Buchan
John Burroughs
John Cournos
John F. Kennedy
John Gay
John Glasworthy
John Habberton
John Joy Bell
John Kendrick Bangs
John Milton
John Philip Sousa
John Taintor Foote
Jonas Lauritz Idemil Lie
Jonathan Swift
Joseph A. Altsheler
Joseph Carey
Joseph Conrad
Joseph E. Badger Jr
Joseph Hergesheimer
Joseph Jacobs
Jules Vernes
Julian Hawthrone
Julie A Lippmann
Justin Huntly McCarthy
Kakuzo Okakura
Karle Wilson Baker
Kate Chopin
Kenneth Grahame
Kenneth McGaffey
Kate Langley Bosher
Kate Langley Bosher
Katherine Cecil Thurston
Katherine Stokes
L. A. Abbot
L. T. Meade

L. Frank Baum
Latta Griswold
Laura Dent Crane
Laura Lee Hope
Laurence Housman
Lawrence Beasley
Leo Tolstoy
Leonid Andreyev
Lewis Carroll
Lewis Sperry Chafer
Lilian Bell
Lloyd Osbourne
Louis Hughes
Louis Joseph Vance
Louis Tracy
Louisa May Alcott
Lucy Fitch Perkins
Lucy Maud Montgomery
Luther Benson
Lydia Miller Middleton
Lyndon Orr
M. Corvus
M. H. Adams
Margaret E. Sangster
Margret Howth
Margaret Vandercook
Margaret W. Hungerford
Margret Penrose
Maria Edgeworth
Maria Thompson Daviess
Mariano Azuela
Marion Polk Angellotti
Mark Overton
Mark Twain
Mary Austin
Mary Catherine Crowley
Mary Cole
Mary Hastings Bradley
Mary Roberts Rinehart
Mary Rowlandson
M. Wollstonecraft Shelley
Maud Lindsay
Max Beerbohm
Myra Kelly
Nathaniel Hawthrone
Nicolo Machiavelli
O. F. Walton
Oscar Wilde

Owen Johnson
P.G. Wodehouse
Paul and Mabel Thorne
Paul G. Tomlinson
Paul Severing
Percy Brebner
Percy Keese Fitzhugh
Peter B. Kyne
Plato
Quincy Allen
R. Derby Holmes
R. L. Stevenson
R. S. Ball
Rabindranath Tagore
Rahul Alvares
Ralph Bonehill
Ralph Henry Barbour
Ralph Victor
Ralph Waldo Emmerson
Rene Descartes
Ray Cummings
Rex Beach
Rex E. Beach
Richard Harding Davis
Richard Jefferies
Richard Le Gallienne
Robert Barr
Robert Frost
Robert Gordon Anderson
Robert L. Drake
Robert Lansing
Robert Lynd
Robert Michael Ballantyne
Robert W. Chambers
Rosa Nouchette Carey
Rudyard Kipling
Saint Augustine
Samuel B. Allison
Samuel Hopkins Adams
Sarah Bernhardt
Sarah C. Hallowell
Selma Lagerlof
Sherwood Anderson
Sigmund Freud
Standish O'Grady
Stanley Weyman
Stella Benson
Stella M. Francis

Stephen Crane
Stewart Edward White
Stijn Streuvels
Swami Abhedananda
Swami Parmananda
T. S. Ackland
T. S. Arthur
The Princess Der Ling
Thomas A. Janvier
Thomas A Kempis
Thomas Anderton
Thomas Bailey Aldrich
Thomas Bulfinch
Thomas De Quincey
Thomas Dixon
Thomas H. Huxley
Thomas Hardy
Thomas More
Thornton W. Burgess
U. S. Grant
Upton Sinclair
Valentine Williams
Various Authors
Vaughan Kester
Victor Appleton
Victor G. Durham
Victoria Cross
Virginia Woolf
Wadsworth Camp
Walter Camp
Walter Scott
Washington Irving
Wilbur Lawton
Wilkie Collins
Willa Cather
Willard F. Baker
William Dean Howells
William le Queux
W. Makepeace Thackeray
William W. Walter
William Shakespeare
Winston Churchill
Yei Theodora Ozaki
Yogi Ramacharaka
Young E. Allison
Zane Grey

www.ingramcontent.com/pod-product-compliance
Lightning Source LLC
Chambersburg PA
CBHW021335250626
47155CB00002B/705